"Only God could win against such invaders."

NO MORE
HIDING

The Biblical Story of Gideon

BETTY NATELSON

Eyewitness

"Grandmother Leah! Grandmother Leah! Tell us a story!"

Grandmother Leah smiles at you. She's not really your grandmother; everyone just calls her that, because she is so old and so wise. "What sort of story would you like?" she asks.

"I want to hear about Judge Gideon," you say. "Rachel says you actually *knew* him. In person!"

Grandmother Leah laughs. "I did know him," she agrees. "I was there when he fought the Midianites—although, of course, I was only a child at the time." Her eyes go distant. "I got into a few adventures of my own, come to think of it."

"Oh, please tell us!" you beg.

"Patience, patience," Grandmother Leah says. "Let me see. Where to begin…"

CHAPTER ONE

Invaders Are Coming!

"Whenever the Israelites planted their crops, the Midianites, Amalekites and other eastern peoples invaded the country." (Judges 6:3)

The blazing sun beat down on Gideon's bent back, sending sweat streaming down his face and arms, but he didn't pause. Grab, swish, slice—another stalk of wheat fell to the earth. Grab, swish, slice. He moved steadily, gripping the stalks of wheat with one hand, swinging his sickle with the other. It was backbreaking work, but there was no time to rest. He had to finish as much as possible before evening came and the Sabbath began.

Grab, swish, slice. Gideon wasn't working alone; a dozen adult servants reaped with him, while the children followed behind. Gideon's eldest son, Jether, walked a few paces behind him. The boy gathered up the fallen stalks of wheat into small bundles. These small bundles would be tied into larger bundles called *sheaves* to dry.

Seven years ago, the Israelites would have then left the sheaves in the open air, and no one would have stolen them. Once dry, the sheaves would have been carted away to the threshing floor, where workers would have loosened the precious wheat grains from the husks and straw.

But nothing was that easy anymore.

"It's almost noon," Jether said, glancing at the sun. "Father, it's almost noon!"

"We'll finish in time," Gideon assured him, although he was far from certain about this. The Midianites sometimes came earlier in the year, sometimes later, but they always came. And once they came, they would steal or destroy everything they found—and kill anyone who stood in their way. "Cheer up," he added. "Maybe they won't come this year."

"They come every year," Jether said. "They always come." There was a sob in the boy's voice, but Gideon didn't have time to stop and console him, not if they wanted to eat next winter. And Gideon knew the price of waiting too long. Last year his second son—Jether's brother—had been killed by raiders who came earlier than expected.

Maybe they would come early again this year.

"It's not fair!" Jether burst out. "This is our land! Grandfather Joash's land! It's been ours for generations! Why do the invaders have to take everything? What have we done to them? We've never hurt them."

"There are evil people in this world," Gideon answered. He meant the words to be calm, but his voice echoed a deep rage. How happy his family had once been, how prosperous! Now, many of his siblings and cousins—and even one of his sons—had been slaughtered by the Midianites, Amalekites, and all the other desert tribes that kept invading them. Gideon remembered the time when his family was safe and well fed. Now they barely had enough food to stay alive.

If that wasn't enough, they were forced to spend their summers hiding in caves like their sheep and cattle—the ones they still had.

Gideon's knuckles went white with anger as he swung his sickle.

"I hate them," Jether growled in a low voice. "I want to kill them all. That's what they deserve. Why doesn't anyone stand up to them? We have to fight!"

Gideon didn't answer, and Jether went on.

"Every year they come, every year since I was a little boy. And we lie down and let them steal everything while we hide in caves! Only after they've crossed back over the Jordan River do we slink out of hiding like snakes from under rocks.

"Why do people let this happen? Are we all cowards? If we fought," he said intensely, "maybe we'd have won. Maybe my brother would still be alive." His voice cracked on the last word.

Despite the time crunch, Gideon could no longer keep his back to his son. He dropped the latest stalk of wheat and turned to embrace the boy. He knew exactly how Jether felt.

The boy leaned into his chest for a minute and then turned away. "We have to get back to work," he said roughly. "Isn't that right?" He plucked the stalk from the ground, not looking at his father.

Gideon didn't move. "I understand, Jether. I understand exactly how you feel. But the truth is that those of us who hid... even though we were sometimes hungry, we survived. I loved your brother, but he should have stayed hidden with us. He was only eleven. He didn't stand a chance against the Midianites and their war camels. No one could have beaten them. He should have listened to our warnings."

"I don't believe no one can beat them," Jether said hotly. "There has to be a way. We can't live like this for the rest of our lives." He glared at Gideon's sickle. "If I had a sword, I'd fight them myself."

"But you don't have a sword," Gideon answered, "so let's

finish harvesting this wheat before the Midianites get here."

Almost before he'd finished his sentence, a cry of alarm made him spin around. It was sixteen-year-old Purah, who had the sharpest eyes and the fastest legs of any of Gideon's servants.

"Look, sir!" the boy cried, pointing frantically.

Gideon followed Purah's finger, alarm flooding his brain. Two figures were approaching on camels from the direction of the Jordan River.

Were the Midianites already on their way?

Without losing a second, Gideon put two fingers in his mouth and whistled a signal. Immediately, every servant in the field ran to join him.

"You see those men on camels?" Gideon called, when everyone was near enough to hear. "They're probably advance scouts for the Midianites. I want to capture them alive."

"Alive!" protested one of the men, a narrow-faced fellow with scars from a fight with some Midianites two years back. "Let's kill them before they kill us!"

"No," Gideon answered firmly. "We don't know who they are. They might be innocent. And if they are Midianites, we need to learn everything they know about the rest of the invaders."

"And then we'll kill them," the narrow-faced man said.

"Yeah, after we teach those desert scum a lesson," another man added, clenching his fists.

"No," Gideon said firmly. He might be the youngest of his brothers, but his father was still the owner of this land, which meant that Gideon was in charge here. And he would make sure things were done right. "We obey God's law. We convict no one without evidence, and we treat strangers fairly. If those men attack you, then defend yourselves and kill them if you have to. But otherwise, we'll take them to the town elders to be questioned and judged."

The servants shifted and looked at one another, but they knew they had to obey Gideon.

Gideon studied the land nearby. He was a farmer, not a soldier, and he'd never set up an ambush before. But he knew he needed a place close by and a plan that all his men understood. He also knew that the Midianites might have already seen them.

That meant he had to trick the Midianites into thinking they'd run away. Now, where to hide?

Of course! There were plenty of dense bushes along the Harod River. The road went beside that river all through the Jezreel Valley. Since his father's farm also lay along the river, Gideon had walked every inch of it many times.

He knew the perfect spot to hide for an ambush: a shady area, thick with trees and bushes. Because it was a pleasant spot on a hot day, the men often ate their noon meal there and left bags of wine in the water to keep them cool.

"Everyone, bring your sickles and follow me," Gideon said. After another quick glance at the approaching camels, he broke into a run. With the others following close behind, he circled away from the river, to where a low hill shielded them from view. Then he led his men around and toward his chosen hiding place.

As he ran, the rest of the plan clicked together in Gideon's mind.

"I've watched these Midianites fight before," he said, when he and his men were squatting down out of sight, recovering their breath. "Sitting up on their camels, they're higher than our heads and as fierce of lions. So we have to trick them into dismounting, and then we have to strike fast. Purah, you spotted them first, so the honor is yours. Lie down over here, near the thickest bushes."

It wasn't just that Purah had the sharpest eyes; he was also one of the bravest among them. And although he was short, he was very fast and very strong. For a job requiring steady nerves and quick reflexes, there was no better choice.

Gideon went on, explaining his plan. "When the Midianites see our wine skins cooling in the river, they'll be tempted to dismount and steal them. But they'll be cautious in case the wine's owner is nearby. That's what Purah's for: he'll pretend to be asleep. These scouts will want to question an Israelite, just like we want to question them. They'll decide it's worth dismounting to get both the wine and an Israelite. So they'll order their camels to kneel. Then we'll strike."

"You mean, once they're off their camels?" Jether asked, giddy at the idea of finally fighting Midianites.

Gideon smiled. "No, we strike while the camels are in the process of kneeling. You've seen the caravans that come through the valley. Did you ever watch a camel kneel?"

Jether laughed in delighted comprehension. "Yeah! They kneel front legs first, while their back legs are still standing. The rider has to hang on to the saddle to keep from pitching over the camel's head. The Midianites won't be able to fight while their camels are half up and half down!"

The others snickered, imagining this. Gideon was glad to hear the laughter, but time was short. He quieted them and pointed out where each would hide. When his servants were in position, he said, "No more talking. Remember, surprise is the key." He himself lay down and shut his mouth, on high alert for the approaching Midianites.

Not far from Purah, Jether crouched behind a dwarf mesquite shrub. He could barely see even Purah through the shrub, let alone the road and river further on—which hopefully meant the Midianites wouldn't be able to see him.

Jether quieted his breath and strained to hear the clip-clop of camel hooves. So far, there was only the hum of insects and the murmur of the gentle water, but any minute—!

His hand hurt from clenching the sickle so hard. He'd never been so excited. At last, he was going to fight Midianites! He smiled as he imagined slaying those vicious enemies with his sickle. His brother would have been amazed at his heroism.

The desire for revenge darkened his eyes and his heart, and his smile fell away. His brother would never get to see his victory. He would be able to boast to his friends about it, but he couldn't bring back the dead. He could only avenge him.

If you hadn't let him go play, maybe he'd still be alive.

No!

If you'd made him listen to Mother and Father... if you had stayed with him and fought alongside him...

Stop it!

Now's your chance to show you aren't a coward... and to avenge him.

Enough!

He shook off his dark thoughts, knowing that revenge was wrong and that he had to focus. What was taking those Midianites so long?

Suddenly he heard it. The sound was muffled at first, but the thumping of camel hooves on hard-packed dirt soon became unmistakable. Then, through the densely packed shrub, Jether saw camel legs: eight legs, tall and thin, with knobbly knees and huge feet. The dwarf mesquite blocked his view of the riders, but he knew they must be there; he could hear their voices.

The two men spoke together softly. Their accents were foreign and all too familiar: Jether had heard those accents each year, when the Midianites came to steal their crops and kill their animals.

Sweat seeped down Jether's face as he waited. The camels stopped about twenty feet from where Purah lay, pretending to sleep. For a moment, there was no sound but the buzzing of insects and the flowing of water. Then Jether heard low murmuring and, finally, sharp, one-word commands to each camel. The camels' knees bent as they began to kneel.

Now! Jether screamed as he surged out of his bush, men on every side of him. Purah leapt to his feet even faster, but other servants were the fastest. They rushed the Midianites. One group piled atop the nearer Midianite, completely blocking him from view.

But where was the other one? There—he had somehow broken through. They couldn't let him get away! Jether was the closest. He should jump forward, swinging his sickle, and stop the man. Be a hero.

But he couldn't move. His eyes went big and round as he stared at the man, sickle drooping in his limp fingers. He had never felt so terrified.

The Midianite moved fast, his eyes wild, his mouth ferocious. Holding high a foot-long double-edged sword, he charged the boy.

Jether stood frozen. He knew he had to move or die, but his muscles wouldn't work. At the last second, as the Midianite swung, he squeezed his eyes shut.

The sword never struck him. After a few breaths, wondering why he wasn't dead, Jether opened his eyes. He saw Purah wrapped around the Midianite's legs. The servant had seen Jether's danger and dived for the Midianite's knees, sending them both sprawling.

Jether's muscles finally let him move, and he sprang back from the Midianite, whose face was inches from his feet.

"Sword!" he yelled, not knowing what he was saying. "Sword!"

The Midianite was scrabbling for his sword, but Purah stomped on the man's fingers and then kicked the sword away. Without pausing, Purah dropped to his knees and wrapped his powerful arms around the man, trapping him with a wrestling hold.

Gideon arrived a moment later, having just tied up the first Midianite. He bound this one too, trussing him up so that he could neither fight nor run away.

When both captured Midianites were kneeling in front of him, helpless, Gideon asked, "Who is your leader?"

The enemy scouts glared hatefully at him. The one Purah had captured raised his chin haughtily and said, "My leader is Zalmunna of the Midianites. Look out, farmer. In two days' time, the first of our men will arrive. You may think you're strong now, but within three days Zalmunna will have your land—and your head."

"We'll see about that," Gideon replied grimly. To four of his servants, he said, "Take them to the town elders, then come back here. We have a harvest to get in."

Jether watched the servants lead their captives away. His hands still shaking from excitement and fear, he felt so ashamed. He was no hero. He was only a thirteen-year-old boy, and he felt useless. With a bowed head he followed his father back to the fields, and he didn't say anything as he gathered the harvested stalks of wheat.

CHAPTER TWO

Buried Treasure

Elsewhere in the valley, on a wall surrounding the crumbled ruins of an ancient building, two nine-year-old boys had plans of their own for the invaders.

"Die, you Midianite!" Benjamin yelled fiercely, throwing a rock with deadly accuracy at an almond tree. "Got him!"

Three sheep trotted nervously away from the tree. The boys were supposed to be watching them—there weren't many sheep left in Israel, because the Midianites kept killing or stealing them, and these were valuable.

Benjamin picked up another stone from his pile and threw it with brutal speed and accuracy at the tree, sending bark flying. "I got another one! He's dead, hah hah!"

"Look out!" cried his friend Samuel. "Their deadliest archer is aiming at us!" He tucked a rock in his slingshot and swung, sending the rock flying at a boulder fifteen feet away. The rock shattered on impact, flinging pieces in every direction. Two more rocks followed, one after the other. "I got him!" Samuel crowed in satisfaction.

The sheep trotted further away.

Benjamin and Samuel stood atop a stone wall. Benjamin was the taller of the two, with straight black hair, brown eyes, and a mischievous grin crooking his lips. Samuel was

11

quieter, but his mind was always in motion.

Both of them had stood on this stone wall many times, playing. It was three feet wide and ten feet high and had been falling apart for centuries. The ground enclosed by the wall's four sides was covered with rubble from a building that once stood there. There were many such ruins in the area, and the boys knew all of them.

"Attack coming!" Benjamin screamed. "To the Stronghold!" Nimble as a squirrel, he scrambled straight down the side of the wall. Samuel rammed his remaining slingshot stones into his leather pouch, then scampered down an easier way and dashed over to join Benjamin.

To get inside the Stronghold, the boys had to squeeze through a crawlspace. Two great blocks of wall had fallen together at an angle. A boy on his belly could just wriggle into the open area underneath. Benjamin went first.

The crawlspace was very dark. After the brightness of the sunshine, the boys were nearly blind and had to find their way by feel. But two body lengths of wriggling got them to the main part of the Stronghold. Here, hidden from outside view, the broken stone blocks didn't quite meet as a ceiling. Daylight streamed into the little room, which was six feet across and high enough to stand up in.

"It's good to be back in our tower," Benjamin said. "We can watch over our city from here and still be safe."

The Stronghold was more like a cave than a tower, really, and not very good for watching sheep, which they were supposed to do every minute. But it was wonderful to have a secret place, one into which adults couldn't follow. Besides, the sheep would be fine. It wasn't like there were any Midianites around.

"Fighting is hungry work," Samuel announced, sitting down on the soft earth and leaning against a smooth rock.

12

He reached into his pouch, pushed his slingshot stones aside, and pulled out the piece of bread his mother had sent with him.

Benjamin, who never stayed still for long (and who had forgotten his own lunch), began idly digging in the dirt with his fingers. "I know!" he said, before Samuel had finished more than a couple of bites. "Let's dig a hole here, just like the storage holes in our houses. That'll protect our food."

He jumped to his feet and began looking around the Stronghold. For the past few weeks, they'd been collecting supplies. One corner was full of sharp rocks to use as weapons against Midianites; another had a variety of twigs and larger hunks of wood to build a fire.

Benjamin picked a sharp stone about the size of his hand and began digging in the middle of the Stronghold while Samuel looked on, chewing the last of his bread.

"Come on, lazy," Benjamin said. "Help me out!"

Hearing the impatience in his friend's voice, Samuel meekly stuffed the rest of his bread in his mouth and got a rock of his own. He hunched next to Benjamin.

"Not here," Benjamin said, exasperated. "You start on that side. We're going to make this hole big."

Samuel scooted over and started scraping the dirt. After a few minutes, during which he wished he could dig as quickly as Benjamin (and that he had brought more lunch), something caught his eye. Something glimmering yellow in the sunlight.

Unable to believe his luck—Benjamin was usually the one to find things—Samuel dug more quickly. He scraped first with the rock, then with his fingers.

"What are you doing?" Benjamin asked irritably, then caught his breath as he saw what Samuel pulled from the ground.

It was a knife sheath, decorated with elegant animals formed out of gold.

Samuel tugged on the knife's hilt and pulled out a slender gold blade ten inches long and slightly leaf-shaped. The hilt had geometric designs and regular bands. It was so narrow that Samuel had no trouble holding it, though his hands were small.

"It's made all out of gold!" he exclaimed, turning it over and over in his hands.

"Let me see!" Benjamin demanded, grabbing for it.

Samuel twisted away. "No, it's mine. I found it."

"I just want to see it," Benjamin insisted. When Samuel didn't respond, he tackled the smaller boy and pried it from his hand. "It's mine too. It was my idea to dig in that corner." He backed away and turned the knife and sheath this way and that, looking at them in amazement.

"I wonder how long this has been buried here. I've never seen one like it." He examined the knife's blade. "Wow, this is *sharp*. It'll dig great." He sat and pressed the tip into the ground.

"Stop!" Samuel cried, too alarmed to be still. "You'll ruin it!"

"No I won't," Benjamin said, scowling. "What stupid kind of knife is ruined by digging?" He tossed it on the ground, not quite giving it back. "I'm tired of digging anyway. I'm going back outside." He slithered back through the tunnel, not waiting for Samuel.

Hardly believing his luck, Samuel picked up the knife and gently wiped off the dirt. He slid it back in its sheath and put the whole thing in his bag. He was tempted to hide it in the cave where no one—least of all Benjamin—would find it and take it from him, but he couldn't bear to let it get dirty again.

Once it was put away, Samuel automatically started after

his friend. But then he hesitated. Benjamin might guess the knife was in his bag. Samuel took it out again and strapped it under his clothing, where no one could see it. Then, with some difficulty, he squirmed back outside.

The sheep raised their heads without much interest when he slithered out. They'd already seen Benjamin head off without his friend, toward the boys' favorite climbing tree.

A couple of miles away, a young girl named Leah hurried down the hillside. She was tall for her age and slender, with skin the color of desert sand and long black hair that never stayed neatly in braids. She was always keeping busy— making bread, playing her reed flute, fetching water, running happily through the fields looking for medicinal herbs... or, like today, looking for her brother.

Leah was often sent to find Benjamin, and she knew the usual places to look, where the grass was plentiful and the sheep content. But normally, she was only looking for him to call him to supper or because the Sabbath would start soon and he needed to get his sheep back before sundown. Only once a year was her errand so great—and so urgent.

Two days before, the Midianites had appeared in Harod Valley. A *maximum* of two days—Leah was too smart to assume that those Midianite scouts had told the truth.

The Midianites scared her. They had come every summer since she'd been five years old—and every year, someone else she knew got killed, her family's crops were stolen, and their house was destroyed.

The invaders didn't only kill adults, either. They even killed children. One of Leah's nightmares was waking up to see a Midianite leaning over her, about to slit her throat.

Leah trotted until she was out of breath, and then kept trotting. She was pretty sure she'd find Benjamin at the spring near the old ruins. She knew every inch of this valley, and that was the best place to watch sheep on a hot day. She hoped she was right; she didn't have time to be wrong.

Leah's mean aunt, the one she'd never liked, used to say, "Be good or I'll sell you to the Midianites." Leah had never been sure if the ill-tempered aunt would actually do that, but she tried to be good, just in case. Right now, though, all that mattered was to be fast.

Leah hurried on, although she was sweating freely. She didn't feel safe in Harod Valley any longer. She wished they had already moved to their cave shelter, where the Midianites couldn't find them.

With these thoughts to drive her on, Leah broke into a run. Long-legged and sure-footed, she ran like a deer—leaping nimbly over small dry creek beds; skidding down the steep, stony side of a ravine; and scrabbling up the hill on the other side. At last, the ruins came into sight. The spring was on the other side and—hopefully—her brother.

Leah skidded around the ruins and stopped, panting, on the other side. Like an oasis on the dry, stony, treeless slope, the sparkling spring bubbled out of the rocks, flowing downhill a dozen feet to a large pool, and from there into a little stream. It wasn't nearly as big as the spring of Harod, which fed a river, but it was Leah's favorite. All around were green grass, trees and bushes, and a small flock of lazy white sheep.

A few feet away, Benjamin and Samuel played. They had crooked sticks in their hands and were swinging them with more enthusiasm than accuracy, obviously sword-fighting.

"Benjamin! Samuel!" she panted, approaching. They glanced her way and then ignored her, continuing their pretend fight.

Leah suddenly realized how hot and thirsty she was. Despite her urgency, she couldn't help herself: she walked past the boys and clambered up to the spring. Kneeling on hands and knees, she lowered her face and let the icy water bubble into her mouth. For a moment, she forgot everything except the pleasure of drinking.

Suddenly, water splashed her face as a pair of nine-year-old feet jumped into the spring.

"Hey!" she cried, jerking away. She wiped the water out of her eyes and glared at Benjamin. He met her eyes and flicked some water at her with his toe. "Stop it!" she cried, already cupping water in her hands and flinging it back at him. Now it was Benjamin's turn to squeak, although he was laughing too hard to mind.

"Catch me if you can!" he told her, and raced down from the spring to the pool, where he jumped in. Leah jumped after him, and Samuel wasn't too far behind. First he splashed Leah and then he splashed Benjamin, and soon it was a free-for-all of laughter and water.

The sheep stared. Humans were so strange.

"Hey, Leah, look at this," Samuel said. It was about twenty minutes later, and the water fight had put him in such a good mood that he forgot his worries over Benjamin stealing his prize. "Amazing, huh?" He unstrapped the golden knife and showed it to her, the soft metal gleaming in the sun.

"Wow," she said, as he handed it over. "This is incredible. Look at how intricate those carvings are! Where'd you find it?"

"It was buried in the—"

Benjamin kicked him, and Samuel swallowed the rest of his sentence. Leah didn't know about the Stronghold. No one but the two boys did; it was their secret.

"—in the dirt," he finished lamely.

"It's amazing," she told him honestly, handing it back.

"I've never seen the like," Samuel said, sounding very superior, "and my father's an expert on metalwork."

A flush of yearning came over Leah. She'd never been to distant lands, where fancy things like this were made. She'd never even been down to the Jordan River.

The Jordan River. Why did that ring a bell? Of course... it was where the invaders had gathered.

The Midianites!

Leah leapt to her feet. "We've got to get going! How could I have forgotten? Father sent me to tell you—the invasion's about to start! We've got to get the sheep safe!"

"Really?" Benjamin asked excitedly. "Wow! I want to see the Midianites. Where are they?"

Faintly regretting he'd brought it out again, Samuel replaced the golden knife in his pouch—there was no use hiding it again, now that Benjamin knew his hiding place.

Unlike his friend, Samuel did not find the Midianites exciting in the least; he found them scary. But he didn't want his friend to tease him, so he put on a brave face. "How do you know when they're coming?"

"Gideon caught two enemy spies today. They said the first of the horde will come up the valley the day after tomorrow. And our lookouts say the Midianite camp is filling up all the space on both sides of the Jordan River." Now everything was coming back to Leah, she deeply regretted her silliness earlier. It felt nightmarish, the way they'd been wasting time. How in the world would they finish everything before the enemy came?

"The day after tomorrow?" Benjamin said, waving away her worries with a laugh. "What's the big rush? We have lots of time!"

Leah fixed him with a stern look. "The Sabbath starts at sundown, or had you forgotten? We have to finish everything before then. Now look at the sun and tell me we have 'lots of time.'"

Instinctively, both boys glanced at the sun and then at each other. It was far later than either of them had realized, and even Benjamin began to feel the urgency—although he wouldn't have admitted it for the world. Instead, he said airily, "So what? There's still lots of time."

Leah set her jaw and turned away from the boys to count the sheep and see how far they'd strayed. She checked and double checked, but her count came out the same each time. "There's a lamb missing."

"No there isn't," Benjamin automatically contradicted.

"Count them yourself."

Samuel scanned his family's flock. The sheep kept moving around, making it hard to count them, but he was sure they were all there.

Benjamin wasn't so lucky. "I don't understand," he complained. "They were all there the last time I counted."

Leah gave him her best Big Sister look. "You didn't watch them the whole time, did you."

"I was here the whole time!" he said defensively—and truthfully. He *hadn't* left. He'd gone inside the Stronghold, sure, and he'd forgotten about the sheep for long stretches, but it wasn't like he'd wandered off.

Leah must have guessed more than he told her, because she crossed her arms and scolded him. "Watching the sheep is your job! You know we can't afford to lose a single lamb. Especially not with the Midianites on the way!"

"It's not my fault," Benjamin maintained stubbornly. "The stupid thing must have wandered off."

"Anyway," Samuel interrupted, seeing Leah was readying herself for a yelling fit, "we can find it now. It can't have gone far."

Leah opened her mouth to say something sarcastic, then stopped. Being mean wouldn't help anything. Now was a time for thinking, not for anger.

She shook her head. "It's more important for us to get the rest of the flock up to the hideout. We barely have time for that. Searching is out of the question—you know that finding a lost lamb can take hours."

Benjamin went white with fear. "But what will Mother and Father say?"

"That's your problem."

"But—but if they notice—you'll tell them it was your idea, right? To come back with the flock instead of looking."

Leah laughed. "You mean, get in trouble for you because you were too lazy to watch the sheep. Not a chance! But," she added judiciously, "I won't *tell* them you lost one, either. Maybe you'll get lucky, and they won't notice. Then we can sneak down here first thing on Sunday, when the Sabbath's over, and I'll help you find it. Okay?"

"I guess," Benjamin said. He figured it was the best he could hope for. To prove none of this bothered him, and that he didn't really believe he'd done anything wrong, he scooped up a stone and hurled it against a rock. It cracked and bounced away. "Midianites, wow!" he cried.

Four sheep skittered further away.

CHAPTER THREE

Altar to an Idol

"The Israelites did evil in the eyes of the LORD,
and for seven years he gave them into the hands
of the Midianites." (Judges 6:1)

Saturday morning dawned gray and chilly, the sunlight creeping through heavy clouds to fall upon the side of Mount Gilboa.

From below, the mountain looked uninhabited. It sloped upward from the valley in a gentle swoop to its rounded top. Its large areas of brown dirt and rock gave way to even larger tree-covered patches, green and fuzzy in the distance. To an enemy standing in the valley, it would seem he could see every part of the mountain. He never would guess that hundreds of people could be hiding there, completely invisible.

Which was what the Israelites counted on.

The cave in which Gideon slept had an opening at one end, like a giant's parted lips. Grass and shrubs surrounded the cave's mouth and clung to the mottled stone. At its tallest, the opening spread high enough for a short man to pass through without ducking, and its total width was three times that. This cave mouth wasn't small, but it was tucked up into

21

the mountain, looking like just another shadow on the rocks.

None of the pallid morning sunlight crept into the cave mouth, and Gideon slept later than usual. He allowed himself to, because there was no work for anyone to do today—not his family or his servants or even his animals. All the work had been finished the day before. Today was the Sabbath, dedicated to worshiping God.

Gideon's family followed the same Sabbath routine as always, with one difference. Now, they stayed clustered in Mount Gilboa's hidden caves or among sheltering rock formations, hidden from enemy eyes.

Every Sabbath morning, Gideon and his family relaxed together and then joined the rest of the community to worship God with words, music, and prayer. In the afternoon, they gathered with his father, Joash, along with Gideon's brothers and sisters and their families.

Gideon enjoyed his work during the week, but he savored the Sabbath as a time to think about his family, his people... and, most importantly, to worship God.

Smiling to himself in anticipation, Gideon rolled over and stretched out his limbs. He enjoyed the luxury of this moment. Beside him, his wife shifted sleepily. "I'm going to take a look around outside, to make sure everything's all right," he murmured to her, and her drowsy noises told him she understood.

Trying not to disturb her, Gideon climbed to his feet and pulled on his best clothing—his best, to honor the Sabbath. By the time he headed outside, the pale sunlight had brightened and warmed into a soft golden glow that made everything beautiful.

Standing at the cave mouth, Gideon surveyed the land, looking for danger. He inhaled the fresh air, slightly damp with morning dew, and let it invigorate him.

He wasn't the only one awake; another man stood at the edge of a cave, some way off. This man looked like an older, stouter version of Gideon. He had the same broad shoulders, the same exceptional height. His hair and beard were pure white, but his brown eyes were as keen as his son's.

When he spotted Gideon, he waved, and each man picked his way across the rocks to meet the other halfway.

"Father!" Gideon called.

"Gideon!" Joash replied, and hurried across the remaining land to bear hug his son.

Gideon kissed his father respectfully. Aside from being his father, Joash of the Abiezrite clan was an important man in their village, Ophrah.

Gideon respected his father as much as everyone else did, and was always happy to see him. But what was he doing out so early?

Gideon burned to ask, but good manners dictated that they talk lightly for several minutes on family matters. Only then could they come to the heart of the matter.

Joash observed, "You did a good job catching those Midianite spies yesterday."

Gideon preened under the praise. It meant more coming from his father than from anyone else.

Joash went on, "I called together the elders, and we interrogated the spies. They've stuck to their story: the invasion will begin tomorrow."

Gideon nodded grimly. He wasn't surprised, but it was still bad news. "We'll have to prepare," he said.

"I agree," said Joash. "That's why some of us are going up to Baal's altar today."

"The altar!" Gideon exclaimed, absolutely flabbergasted. "But—but—today's the Sabbath!" It was the only thing he could think of to say. He knew that Joash sometimes

23

worshiped at Baal's altar, which was bad enough, but to break the Sabbath—the LORD's day—to worship there—it was unbelievable! It went against everything he had been taught.

"Don't act so shocked," Joash said, annoyed. "You know we can't wait—the invasion is coming tomorrow. We must make a sacrifice to Baal to ask for his help. Your brother Judah has already promised to bring his family, and I want you to bring yours. We need your public support to give our people hope."

Joash may have phrased this as a request or desire, but his tone told Gideon it was an order—an order from his father, whom the Ten Commandments told him he must honor.

Something broke inside Gideon's heart. He knew—had known for years—that Joash sometimes worshiped Baal, that he made sacrifices. But part of him had never exactly *believed* it. Surely his good, upright, and honorable father wouldn't bow down to hunks of stone and wood. Surely he wouldn't disobey the true God's commandments.

Gideon swallowed hard. He loved his father and he respected him, but Joash was only human, and that meant he could do wrong... and what he was doing was very, very wrong.

What his father was doing was evil.

Gideon's hands trembled. This was harder than facing down Midianites on camels. But he had to do it. He had to try to make his father understand.

He licked his lips. "Father, you know the Ten Commandments. Grandmother Miriam taught them to you as she taught them to me. How can you worship other gods and bow down to their idols? How can you break the Sabbath to do this?"

Joash clicked his tongue in disgust and frustration, as if Gideon were the one who didn't understand. "Ophrah's just a little village of farmers, son. You ask how I can break the Sabbath to ask for help—help we'll die without. I ask how I could do anything else."

Gideon answered, "You could do the one thing that might actually help: obey the LORD God and ask *Him* to save us! He could actually do something—Baal can't. It's thanks to the LORD's help that we have this 'little village of farmers' at all. He's the one who has saved Israel over and over again!"

"Yes, yes, I know the stories," Joash said, waving his hand dismissively. "The LORD helped Moses and Joshua and Deborah and all the rest. But that was a long time ago, and the great Judges are all dead. What does it matter that the LORD helped them way back when? We need help *tomorrow*."

Joash gazed down the rocky, shrubby hillside to the valley far below.

"I've worked my whole life on that farm," he said, a wisp of sadness in his voice. "It's all I have. It's all I will leave to my children—what's left of it. There are my crops, my sheep, my cattle. And in a few days, most of it will be destroyed—just as it was last year and the year before that and the year before that, going back seven years."

The weary softness in his face sharpened into something hard and ugly. "I'll do whatever it takes to protect it. That farm's more important to me than anything else—even the Ten Commandments. Even my own life. So yes, I will worship Baal and make sacrifices to him on the Sabbath. The Baal altar was built on a hilltop on my land; it will protect what I own."

Gideon shook his head. When had his father gone wrong? When had Joash started worshiping not only Baal, but also his farm and his crops—when he should have been

25

worshiping only the LORD God?

What could Gideon do now?

He said, "But the Baal altar can't protect you. It couldn't even protect itself. Grandmother Miriam says that altar's the reason God lets the desert tribes take over our land. If you want to save us, you should get rid of it, not go worship at it."

"What's this?" a new voice intruded. It was Ahab. Like Joash, he was a village elder; but unlike him, he was only half Israelite. His other half was Amorite, and on that side of the family, he had grown up with Baal worship. Gideon knew that one of Ahab's dreams was to have the whole village—Israelite and Amorite—fully enmeshed, so that everyone worshiped the LORD and Baal equally. Really, Ahab couldn't see any difference between them.

Gideon drew back slightly, wary. He knew how vicious Ahab could get when crossed, but Gideon also didn't want to back down.

"Did I hear you suggest we get rid of Baal's altar?" Ahab snarled. "How dare you, you—you blasphemer! That altar is sacred. You should be whipped for speaking that way."

Gideon looked to his father, but Joash made no move to defend his son. So Gideon squared his shoulders, hands on hips. If arguing with Ahab would get Joash to listen, that's what he should do. He knew he was right, and he knew this was too important to back down from. This discussion wasn't just about his father or his family: this was about protecting all Israelites by obeying God's commandments.

Gideon pitched his voice to be firm but not aggressive. "The LORD God parted the Red Sea," he said. "He broke down the walls of Jericho. He created the Earth and Sun and stars and brought Noah through the flood.

"What has Baal done? You can't show me a single

thing... because Baal is nothing more than a helpless, powerless, unliving pile of rocks."

Ahab's face flushed with fury and he stepped closer, fists clenched. He looked like he wanted to hit Gideon. Maybe he would. It wouldn't be the first time—although it would be the first time since Gideon had reached manhood. Ahab must know he was too old and frail to win a fight against the young man.

Gideon was too honorable to attack an elder, but would defend himself if he needed to. Ahab must have realized this, because he did not strike with his fists. Instead, he hissed, "You are the one who is helpless and powerless. You're a youngest son, which means you are nothing even to your own family—and your family leads the weakest clan in Manasseh. Tomorrow when the Midianites attack and the rest of us fight, where will you be? Standing here and watching and doing nothing, like a coward. So keep your mouth shut and don't go telling the real men what to do."

"Now, now, let's have peace," Joash said belatedly, raising his hands and making his best attempt at a smile. "Let's not bicker. Remember, we are not enemies—our enemies are the Midianites."

Gideon kept his jaw clenched shut. He agreed that the Midianites were their enemies... but he also knew that Baal was God's enemy. And it looked like Ahab might be his.

Joash looked to his son. "Come on, Gideon," he said. "We are only common, ordinary farmers. We may not be able to do much, so let us do what we can. Today, as a family, we will go to my Baal altar and sacrifice a bull. Then tomorrow, he may help us."

"I agree that we should do what we can," Gideon responded. "And what we can do is obey God's law and tear down that evil altar."

"Your boy is slow, Joash," said Ahab. "He doesn't learn. That's going to get him killed someday."

Gideon didn't pause, and he didn't give an inch. "God gave us laws *because* we are only common, ordinary farmers. His laws tell us what He wants us to do, and that's what we should do."

His father shrugged and sighed. "It's more complicated than that, Gideon."

"Is it?" Gideon replied. "Tell me, Father: if Ahab told you to steal something, would you do it?"

"What happened to not making false accusations?" snapped Ahab, offended. "I'm no thief!"

"Why not?" Gideon asked.

His father looked at him like he was crazy. "Because it's wrong!"

"And how do you know it's wrong? Because God's law says so. Well, God's law also says not to worship other gods."

"It's not the same," Joash said weakly, although he knew it was exactly the same. He shook himself. He didn't want to think about that, because it made him feel guilty. "Look, we no longer live in the olden days. We aren't just Hebrews anymore, following Moses across the desert. Here in Ophrah, we live among the Amorites. We have to get along with them. We can't just say our God is right and theirs is wrong. They wouldn't like it!"

"They wouldn't *like* it?" Gideon cried. "Our God is the king of the universe. Theirs is a pile of rocks. Are we going to sacrifice the truth—and ourselves—because we are afraid they won't *like* it?"

"You are a stupid, ignorant young man," Ahab said scornfully. "I am half Amorite, so I know. Worshiping Baal has been part of my family's tradition for generations, and it's a good tradition. That's why the Hebrews have started doing it, too."

"It's an evil tradition, and Hebrews have started doing it because they've started falling into evil."

Ahab's anger had deepened into something dark and still. He no longer snapped or clenched his fists; he only looked at Gideon with contempt and loathing. When he spoke again, it was to deliver a threat: "Don't think I'll forget this, boy. Don't think Baal will, either."

"Peace," Joash said again, not liking where this was going. "Gideon, this is an order. You will come with us to the sacrifice, and you will participate."

Gideon shook his head. "Today, my family and I will keep the Sabbath holy, worshiping the one true God."

"What an obedient son," Ahab murmured to Joash, maintaining his quiet, deep loathing.

His words did their job: they drove Joash into a rare fury. "If you will not obey me like a son in the morning," he warned Gideon, "then you will not be welcome in my home in the afternoon."

Gideon did not answer for a long moment; he didn't trust himself to. He felt so betrayed, so hurt, that he was afraid of saying something angry in return.

Joash didn't wait for Gideon to recover. He stomped back to his cave. With one last sarcastic look, Ahab left also.

Tears in his eyes, Gideon watched them go. When they were too far to hear, he murmured to himself, "Would you have me obey my father over my God? Oh, beloved father—what has happened to you?"

CHAPTER FOUR

A Message Delivered

"Midian so impoverished the Israelites that they
cried out to the LORD for help." (Judges 6:6)

The children couldn't help but sense how worried and tense
the adults felt, but it was too pleasant a day to worry much.
So while Joash huddled in conference with the other leaders
at one end of the clearing, and the other adults clustered to
worry and gossip at the other, the children played in the
middle.

The villagers met every Sabbath morning for a worship
meeting. This clearing was a relatively safe location: a sunken
area hidden from below by a natural grouping of boulders.
Benjamin dismissed the adults' worry as silly. How could
anyone feel afraid, hugged by the mountain like this?

"Catch me if you can!" he called to Samuel, and led his
friend in a wild chase across the grass and up a boulder taller
than a grown man.

While Samuel panted and tried to keep up, Benjamin bal-
anced precariously and eyed the gap to the next boulder. If
he aimed right, and used his momentum—perfect.

Benjamin leapt across the deep crack and landed safely,

four feet away and several feet lower. Without pause, he leapt again, over another gap, to an even lower stone. That one was close enough to the next that he could half-spring, half climb up to a new, higher perch.

He stopped, crouching, and grinned back at Samuel. The adults liked to gripe about having to spend their summers up here, but he loved it.

Samuel didn't feel nearly so confident. He didn't like the look of those gaps between boulders or the thought of missing a jump and skinning his knees as he tumbled down. On the other hand, cuts and bruises were nothing compared to how Benjamin would mock him if he didn't try. So, following his friend's example, he jumped down to the first rock and used his momentum to spring over to the next.

He caught himself awkwardly, sandal sliding off. Desperately, Samuel clung to the boulder and pulled himself upright. He could feel the gap yawning beneath him, but he didn't let himself fall. With a great effort, he pulled himself upright and, trying not to think about it too hard, crossed to the final boulder and joined Benjamin at the top. "I made it," he told his friend.

"But I did it first," said Benjamin.

Down below, Leah rolled her eyes at this exchange. *Typical*, she thought. *Boys.*

She had other interests, and now was the perfect time to go talk with Grandmother Miriam.

Old Grandmother Miriam sat as comfortably as her ancient body would allow. The sun warmed her favorite seat, a naturally smooth, chair-shaped stone, and eased her aches and pains, of which she had many. No one knew exactly how old she was—the joke was that she had crossed the desert with Moses—but everyone called her "grandmother." Though her body was old, her mind retained a full knowledge of the history and the laws of the people, and she was loved for her kindness and her wisdom. Today, she had brought small honey cakes for all the children.

"I've been looking for the herbs you taught me about," Leah told her, perching beside her. "Look." She held out a spiky aloe leaf. "I got it for your joints."

Grandmother Miriam took the leaf with weathered, worn fingers. Though her body had grown frail and thin with age, and though her joints ached with the weather and her bones creaked, those fingers remained steady and strong. "You are a good girl, Leah," she said. The words were simple, but deep emotion lay under them. "Have you found anything else?"

Leah nodded vigorously. "I found loads of horehound for digestion, too. Every time I walk outdoors, I look for more plants. But I couldn't remember how to find...what was it called? The one for fever."

"Anise," Grandmother Miriam said, the multitudinous lines on her face creasing around her smile. "That plant likes full sun and well-drained soil, but it also wants to be protected from the wind. You've probably seen it without realizing what it was. It'll be easier to spot in summer, when it blooms in clumps of dozens of white flowers."

"*That's* anise?" Leah exclaimed. "But I've seen that loads of times!"

Grandmother Miriam patted Leah's head, which would have annoyed the girl if anyone else had done it. "That's often the way with these things," she said. "Don't worry about it: you're a quick study, and I'm happy to teach you. I want you to learn all the herb medicine I know while I'm still alive to teach you. Someday, you will be healer in my place. You already know more about it than almost anyone in the village, and this knowledge is important."

Leah took the compliment, but she replied, worried, "You're not going to…to die, are you?"

Grandmother Miriam laughed. "Not soon, I hope. But everyone dies eventually, and so I don't want to put off teaching you. You may know a lot, but there's a lot more to learn!"

Leah bit her lip and nodded. She was saved from having to answer by Samuel and Benjamin, who threw themselves down at Grandmother Miriam's feet.

Leah wrinkled her nose at the boys' dirty faces and scraped hands, but she was grateful for the distraction. She didn't like thinking about Grandmother Miriam dying.

"Give us some sweets!" Benjamin begged.

"Oh, please!" said Samuel. "We know you have honey cake."

"And you know you've already had some," Grandmother Miriam said, laughing and giving them each a second piece. "Don't you go licking your filthy fingers now," she added, when Samuel started doing exactly that.

"Sorry," Samuel said guiltily, cramming the rest of the cake in his mouth.

Grandmother Miriam chuckled. "Oh, you," she said, and gave him another piece. "Now, have you collected any new treasures recently?"

Benjamin rolled his eyes and snagged another cake before heading off to see if he could find another boy to play with. But Samuel glowed.

"I sure have," he said proudly. All his possessiveness around Benjamin and Leah evaporated in front of Grandmother Miriam. He trusted her not only to not take his treasure, but to protect it from being taken by anyone else. Even Benjamin respected Grandmother Miriam, although he was irreverent about almost everyone else.

Heart beating rapidly in anticipation, Samuel drew the knife out of its place of honor in his pouch. Its golden sheath gleamed under the midday sun, glinting off the carvings and sending reflected light to dance on his fingers.

Balancing the knife across both his hands, Samuel lifted it reverently to Grandmother Miriam.

Grandmother Miriam lay her aloe leaf across her lap so she could lean forward and, with a look for permission, pick up the knife with as much care as Samuel could have wished. She turned it over slowly, examining the markings, and then drew it from its sheath. The more she looked, the more her eyes lit up with interest, and the more her whole body thrummed with excitement and energy.

"Why," she said, in an amazed whisper, "it's an old Egyptian knife. I haven't seen one like this in years. Decades." She brought the blade close to her ancient eyes, the better to see it. "This must be about two hundred years old, from the reign of the pharaoh Ramses."

"Wow," Samuel breathed in wonder, and even Leah had stopped fiddling with her skirt to lean in. She didn't usually find Samuel's treasures interesting, but the foreign knife had struck her interest. Besides, even Grandmother Miriam was impressed! "I wonder why it's in Ophrah," he went on. "Egypt's a long way away."

"I bet a caravan sold it here," Leah guessed.

"Maybe so," Grandmother Miriam agreed. "Then again, this part of Canaan was controlled by the Egyptians in those days. The owner of this knife may have been an officer stationed here. It's an elegant knife, more decorative than for everyday use, although he might have used it too. He was probably very proud of it."

"Wow," Samuel said again, awed by the knife anew as Grandmother Miriam handed it back to him. "Is it real gold?"

"Oh, yes. Or the handle is. The blade is bronze, of course—gold would be too soft for a knife edge. Either way, this is a very valuable knife. Take good care of it." She watched Samuel curiously as he slid it back in his pouch twice as carefully as he'd taken it out. "You found it in the ruins by the spring?"

"Yeah," he said, and didn't add anything else. Not even Grandmother Miriam knew about the Stronghold, and he intended to keep it that way.

Benjamin jogged back up to them, looking bored and annoyed. None of the other children could come play right then and he needed something to do. "Come on," he ordered Samuel. "Let's play King of the Boulder!"

Samuel jumped up, glad he'd already tucked his treasure away. "See you later!" he told Grandmother Miriam, and dashed off after his friend.

Leah didn't waste this reprieve: she went right back to pumping Grandmother Miriam for information about herbs and medicines. They were just digging into the benefits and dangers of stinging nettle when Gideon burst into the clearing, shouting for attention.

"A prophet of the LORD has come!" he cried. "He wants to speak to the whole town!"

"A prophet?" said Joash. "Which one?"

"What's his name?" asked another.

"Where's he from?"

"What does he want to say?"

"I don't know!" Gideon said, a touch exasperated. "You'll need to ask him. He's waiting below, on the speaking rock."

"Is he going to help us?" villagers asked one another. "Is the LORD going to save us from the Midianites?" Even the

Amorites were getting excited about the prospect, but the Israelites felt as worried as they were eager. Prophets didn't always bring good news.

"Help me up, Leah," Grandmother Miriam said, creaking as she leaned on the girl. "I'm not as spry as I once was."

"Yes, of course," Leah said, bracing herself. Grandmother Miriam moved around well enough on her own, given plenty of time, but hurrying was hard for her. "But I don't understand," Leah went on, when they'd taken the first few steps. "What's he here for?" And then, because she'd often heard about prophets but never had them properly explained, added, "What exactly *is* a prophet? What does he do? Why's he so important?"

"A prophet is a person who speaks God's word to us," the wise old woman answered.

"You speak His word."

"I relate what the Lord has said in the past—as is written down in Scripture. Prophets tell us what God is saying *now*. Sometimes—let's go around that rock, dear; it looks unstable—sometimes, a prophet tells us what we should do or what we're doing wrong, and sometimes he or she tells us what is going to happen in the future."

A distant expression came to Grandmother Miriam's cloudy eyes. "I saw a prophet once—the great Judge Deborah. Right after the big battle. You must listen carefully to what this prophet says now."

Leah had heard the story of Deborah many times. She wanted to press to hear it again, but all too soon, they came to the Overlook.

The speaking rock on which the prophet stood was a boulder at the edge of the Overlook. The hill spread upward from the rock as a natural miniature amphitheater. People could easily sit and stand on the hillside and hear the speaker with little effort—but no one far below could hear what was going on. Since sound travels up, speakers always stood lower than their crowd.

Leah didn't know what she'd expected the prophet to look like. If pressed, she might have imagined a woman, like Deborah, maybe old and wise like Grandmother Miriam. But this one was a man, and his hair was brown instead of white. He looked ragged and worn and dusty from traveling a long road.

Still, there was something about him. He had presence; just being near him was thrilling.

Some villagers peppered the prophet with questions, but he didn't answer them. He hardly said anything until the whole village of Ophrah had gathered before him. Then he didn't waste time introducing himself or engaging in polite small talk; he got right to business.

Pitching his voice so everyone could hear, he proclaimed: "This is what the LORD, the God of Israel, says: I brought you up out of Egypt, out of the land of slavery. I snatched you from the power of Egypt and from the hand of all your oppressors. I drove them from before you and gave you their land. I said to you, 'I am the LORD your God; do not worship the gods of the Amorites, in whose land you live.' But you have not listened to me."

The prophet stopped. He looked sternly, first at one person and then at another. He frowned at Joash and finished, "That is the word of the LORD."

This announcement was not what people wanted to hear. They shifted and murmured to one another. Several voices rose in anger, but the prophet didn't wait for responses, and he didn't answer questions. He simply turned around, climbed down from the rock, and left. A couple of younger men chased after him, and the prophet turned and spoke quietly to them. But it was clear that whatever he said was as unsatisfactory as what had come before, and they came back muttering unhappily.

"Is that... it?" Leah asked Grandmother Miriam, who was sitting on the ground beside her.

"Oh, yes," said Grandmother Miriam, looking troubled but not surprised.

"It didn't sound very nice." What a vast understatement! Leah felt like crying. "When he said 'the gods of the Amorites,' what did he mean? Baal?"

"Certainly. Baal, Asherah—all of them."

Disturbed, almost shivering, Leah looked to the clumps of arguing adults. "But what did he mean?" she asked. "He didn't tell us what we should do or what will happen in the future! He only told us about the past and about now."

Grandmother Miriam shook her head. "I'd say he told us both," she said. "He told us what we are doing wrong—worshiping the Amorite gods—and what we should do—stop. He told us that God isn't going to rescue us as long as Baal's altar stands... as long as anyone in the village worships the false Amorite gods. And I daresay that means He *will* rescue us if we come back to Him."

Leah hugged her arms around her knees and rocked forward. Gideon's son Jether, who was standing nearby, asked Grandmother Miriam, "Why does my grandfather Joash keep the Baal altar anyway?"

Grandmother Miriam crooked her finger for him to come closer, and he sat with them. "I've known Joash since he was a baby," she said. "He was always a good boy, but he had one flaw: he wanted everyone to like him. Oh yes, that can be a flaw, when it's too important to you. You see, when his Amorite friends wanted him to put up that altar, he didn't think he could say no. He thought that being *nice* was more important than being *good.*"

She huffed out a breath, part sad and part irritated. "Now he and his sons worship at that altar—all, Jether, except your father. And I fear for them. It is an evil thing, to worship a false god. And you heard the prophet—it is the reason the LORD hasn't saved us."

Leah didn't know what to say. Joash wasn't her grandfather, but she had been taught to respect him. Her parents always spoke well of him. What if they started worshiping Baal too? What if they wanted *her* to go to the altar? What would she do?

Secretly, she promised herself that if anyone tried to make her worship Baal, she'd run straight to Grandmother Miriam for help.

"I wish people would just do what's right and stop being so awful," Jether said miserably, hugging his knees.

Grandmother Miriam drew him into a half-hug. These children had already suffered so much unhappiness in their lives—and, she suspected, would endure much more in the future—that she couldn't bear to see them waste this fine day in fear. "You children go play," she said. "It's the Sabbath. You'll have plenty of time for work and worry tomorrow. Go on with you."

Besides, she told herself, *I want to talk with the leaders and hear what they're saying about the prophet's message. I don't trust them to understand it correctly.*

CHAPTER FIVE

Chosen to Lead

"Go and save Israel. Am I not sending you?"
(Judges 6:14)

Gideon didn't even wait for the sun to rise. The next morning, in the dark before the dawn, he gathered his servants. Together, they fumbled their way down to the valley and arrived at the field as the first light touched the morning sky.

The air chilled their skin, wicking away moisture and stealing breath, but hard work would soon cure that. Every man knew what was at stake: either they threshed the wheat and carried it to the secret storage places on the mountain, or the Midianites would steal their crops and the Israelites would go hungry.

They got to work with only a few short instructions. Men ran to the bundles of dry, harvested wheat and carried them to the threshing floor. There, some men drove ox-pulled sledges to separate the wheat kernels from the straw, while the others gathered up more bundles. After the wheat kernels were separated, the men carried them up the mountain.

It was hard work, made worse by the constant knowledge that at any moment, the Midianites might be upon them. There was no singing this morning, no jokes. The men simply did what had to be done.

As before, Jether worked with his father. He sweated and ached and trembled in anticipation of a messenger. Then the moment came, the moment he'd been fearing: an Israelite galloping toward them at top speed on one of their few, precious horses:

"The Midianites are coming! The Midianites are coming!" the messenger shouted. "They've crossed the Jordan River!"

"All right, men," Gideon ordered, "let's get this last cart of wheat to safety."

He had trained his servants well, and they trusted him. No one panicked, although faces were strained and breathing short. Jether hurried along with the others, salvaging all the wheat they could. He almost cried, seeing how much they had to leave behind.

Gideon had much the same thought. "I'm not turning over one more grain of wheat to the invaders than I have to," he said grimly. "Jether, I'm putting you in charge of the carts. Get them up to safety and stay there. Purah, you and I are taking these wheat bundles to the winepress. We'll finish what we can there."

"The winepress?" Purah asked, puzzled. "Oh, I get it!" Grapes weren't in season, so the Midianites wouldn't think to look inside the winepress. Not only that, but the grapevines—planted in dense rows ten feet apart—would help hide them from view. Best of all, since the grapes grew on the lower hillsides, they would be close to the safety of Mount Gilboa. It was a brilliant plan, although not without risk.

But going hungry was risky, too.

41

Purah and Gideon piled wheat bundles into the last cart and dragged it to the winepress. They passed the stone watchtower at the edge of the vineyard and the low stone wall meant to keep wild boars and other beasts from trampling the grapes. Then they went through the rows of growing grapes until, finally, they came to the winepress.

Gideon's grandfather had cut two levels of the wine press out of solid rock, and although Midianites had trampled through it, they'd never substantially damaged it.

While Purah spread out the grain in the wine press, Gideon went to the top level. This was a flat, shallow pit eight feet across and knee deep, sloping gently downhill. From here, he could see the valley. Unfortunately, people from the valley would be able to see him, too. If anyone came near, he'd jump into the smaller, deeper pit below. During grape season, that lower pit would be full of the juice from crushed grapes, but right now, it was dry.

"Thank you for your hard work," he told Purah. "Go now to safety. I'll do the threshing myself."

Purah drew himself up, offended. "I'm not afraid to stay, sir. And if the Midianites come, you'll need my help."

Gideon shook his head. "I'm not questioning your strength or spirit, Purah. You've proven over and over again that you're brave. That's why I'm giving you this important task: go back to the caves and defend our people. Besides, two men down here will be twice as easy for the enemy to see. I'll be safer alone."

Purah still didn't like this, but it made sense. Besides, he was a servant. It was his duty to obey. "Yes, sir," he said reluctantly. "But stay safe, won't you?"

Gideon grinned. "I'll do my best."

He wasn't too worried—yet. The messenger had ridden here at top speed; armies took a lot longer to move, even armies mounted on camels. He doubted the Midianites would arrive before nightfall. Hiding in the winepress was more to avoid the sharp eyes of scouts than to evade the main force. He wasn't safe, but he wasn't in that much danger—yet.

It was strange, Gideon reflected, beating the grain until the kernels were separated, to be completely alone like this. Usually, being alone didn't bother him; the heat and concentration of backbreaking work was enough to distract him. But today was different. The air stood still, without the usual noonday breeze. No insects buzzed their wings; no birds called to one another. The earth was waiting. And though he was sweating, Gideon felt cold.

A shadow fell in front of him, as though a piercing light suddenly shone behind his back. Gideon whirled around in terror, dropping his threshing branch—and caught his breath.

Only six feet away stood a man. A strange man holding a staff. Or was it a man? His face was bright as lightning, and his eyes glowed like torches. A pure white linen robe clothed him, and a belt of gold cinched his waist.

This was no Midianite. This was an angel of the Lord.

Words stuck in Gideon's throat; not even a croak emerged.

In a voice like the chorus of many voices, the angel spoke: "The LORD is with you, mighty warrior."

Gideon stared and trembled. His mouth had gone dry and his mind blanked. But the angel was waiting for him to reply. He had to say something. And so, too shocked to think properly, he spoke to the angel as he would to his father—which is to say, he argued. "But sir," he said, "if the LORD is with us, why has all this happened to us? Where are all his wonders that our fathers told us about when they said, 'Did not the LORD bring us up out of Egypt?' But now the LORD has abandoned us and put us into the hand of Midian."

Although he was arguing out of habit, Gideon really did want to know the answer. He had wondered about this for seven years. True, there had been that prophet yesterday, talking to them about the gods of the Amorites... but the elders had argued about the meaning of that prophecy, mostly because they hadn't liked it, and he had ended up more confused than enlightened.

The angel didn't directly answer Gideon's question. Instead, the LORD spoke through the angel's mouth, saying, "Go in the strength you have and save Israel out of Midian's hand. Am I not sending you?"

Hearing the LORD speak through the angel was even more alarming than speaking with the angel. Never for a moment did Gideon question Who was speaking; he simply knew. God was talking to him directly... and telling him, Gideon, to go out and save Israel.

Hold on a minute. Save Israel? Him? Gideon was a farmer, not a soldier—not a "mighty warrior." It hardly seemed possible that God would make a mistake, but if it was possible, then Gideon would think that God had mixed him up with someone else. Anyone else.

He cleared his throat and tried to put it politely. "But LORD," he said, "how can I save Israel? My clan is the weakest in Manasseh, and I am the least in my family."

Again, the LORD spoke through the angel: "I will be with you, and you will strike down all the Midianites together."

This... certainly wasn't what Gideon had expected when he had prayed to the LORD for help. Like the other villagers, he had many times asked God to raise up a leader to destroy the Midianites. But he hadn't had himself in mind!

That thought made him wonder something else. Since he wasn't a warrior, and since God would surely choose a warrior... what if it wasn't really God who was talking to him?

What if this stranger wasn't an angel? What if it was something else, some other being with a glowing face and flaming eyes? What if it was a demon in disguise—or even a Midianite spy? How would Gideon know? It wasn't like he had experience with this sort of thing.

Gideon searched his memory. If his own experiences wouldn't help him, maybe the Scriptures would. What did they say about meetings with angels?

Of course! "If I have now found favor in your eyes," he told the LORD, "give me a sign that it is really you talking to me. Please do not go away until I come back and bring my offering and set it before you."

The LORD answered, "I will wait until you return."

Heart and mind racing, Gideon hurried up the mountain. What would be a proper offering to the LORD? His people mostly ate grains and fruits, saving their livestock to produce hair to weave and milk to drink. That being said, they did offer meat to guests and as sacrifices to God.

Preparing a proper offering wasn't a fast process, but if that really was an angel of the LORD below, he'd understand that these things took time—and he had agreed to wait. He'd give Gideon the time he needed to prepare a young goat in a suitable way.

But that wasn't the test. The test was what Gideon's guest did with the offering when Gideon brought it. That would tell Gideon what he needed to know.

Working quickly, Gideon selected a goat in perfect condition and killed it, then prepared the meat for cooking and brought it into his cave.

"Gideon!" his wife cried as he entered. "You're back!" Her eyes fell on the goat. "What's going on?"

"This is something I have to do all by myself," Gideon told her. "I'll explain later. Please stand outside the cave and keep the children and others out. I've got to do everything exactly right."

Filled with hope and wonder, his wife agreed and went outside.

The coals of the fire pit still glowed hot from bread-baking, but even so, it seemed to take forever to build up the fire, set a pot of water over it to heat, and cut up the goat meat into small chunks that would cook quickly.

While the meat boiled, Gideon mixed a bushel of flour with water and oil but no yeast. He would serve his visitor unleavened bread. He shaped the bread into flat, round pieces the size of plates and laid them over the fire.

Once the meat was cooked to perfection, Gideon fished out the pieces and set them in a basket. The broth, he poured into a clay pot. Finally, he took the bread off the fire and placed it into another basket.

All this was an enormous amount of food, enough for a large family. Since it was too bulky and heavy for Gideon to easily carry down to the winepress, he loaded it into a cart to bring down.

As promised, the angel had not left. He was waiting quietly under an oak tree near the wine press, staff in hand. When Gideon neared, the angel told him, "Take the meat and the unleavened bread, place them on this rock, and pour out the broth."

Gideon blinked. He'd never really thought about the rock before, but now that he looked at it, he saw a large block of stone, several feet high and flat on top. It looked almost like an altar, and Gideon realized that that was what the angel wanted him to use it as.

Gideon suddenly felt small and unworthy. First, the angel had called him a mighty warrior and said he would destroy the Midianites. Now, the glowing visitor wanted him to do the work of a priest. Only a priest could place an offering upon an altar. Who was Gideon? Nobody.

But who was Gideon to disobey an angel's order?

Trembling, Gideon took the basket of meat and laid the chunks upon the rock. Then he did the same with the bread. Finally, he took up the heavy earthenware pot of broth and poured it over the food, soaking the bread and meat... just as a priest would do for a sacred offering.

Clutching his hands together nervously, Gideon backed away from the altar.

Without another word, the angel lifted his staff and touched its tip to the meat and unleavened bread.

Searing fire flashed out of the rock. Gideon jumped, his eyes burning from the sudden light, but he never took his eyes off the altar. In moments, the meat and bread had burned up.

Open-mouthed, Gideon turned back to the angel. But as his eyes landed on God's messenger, the angel vanished.

There could be no more questions, no more doubt. This angel had been from God, and the words he had spoken had been God's words.

"Ah, Sovereign LORD!" Gideon cried. "I have seen the angel of the LORD face to face!"

What did this mean? Was he about to drop dead? How could he have seen what he'd seen and live?

A voice like many voices—a voice from the LORD—spoke to him. "Peace!" it said. "Do not be afraid. You are not going to die."

Gideon fell to his knees, head bowed, overwhelmed. This morning, he had been an average farmer; now, he was called to be more. He was to be a warrior and a priest. One day, he would build an altar to the LORD upon that rock and call it

The LORD Is Peace, but that was long in the future. For this moment, he could only submit himself to God.

He didn't know what was coming next. He only knew that whatever the LORD called him to do, that's what he would do.

CHAPTER SIX

Hidden Away

"The Midianites did not spare a living thing....
they invaded the land to ravage it."   (Judges
6:4–5)

There was the lost sheep to consider, and Benjamin wasn't
going to let her forget it for a moment.

Leah had woken up that morning with a rock in her back,
one she'd somehow missed when sweeping out from under
her sleeping mat. She twisted and turned until she could see
the bruise to her satisfaction and conclude what she already
knew: she hated caves.

She hadn't always felt this way. Even last year, hiding
away in the many-pocketed limestone ridge of Mount Gilboa
had been a treat. She had regularly gone exploring with her
best friend, Bithiah, and had liked to boast that she knew the
cave system better than anyone.

Then, one day last year, she and Bithiah had taken oil
lamps and slithered deep inside a cave they hadn't visited in
years. Bithiah had gone first, which had saved Leah's life.

Nothing could save Bithiah's life. Leah had dragged her
away from the nest of venomous mole vipers as quickly as she

49

could, and had half-carried her friend, sobbing all the way, to find Grandmother Miriam. It had taken nightmarish ages to find the old woman, and by the time they had, Bithiah was beyond help.

Grandmother Miriam told Leah not to blame herself, but Leah found this hard. If only Leah hadn't had to search for Grandmother Miriam—if only *she* had known the right herbs to help Bithiah—then maybe Bithiah wouldn't have died.

Hearing Leah blame herself, Grandmother Miriam had looked keenly at the sobbing girl and promised to teach her about herbs, if Leah wished. But the girl would have to work hard and learn quickly and not complain.

Leah had promised she'd do her very best, and she did. She went down by the river and through fields and into wooded areas, carrying out any errand Grandmother Miriam asked.

But she'd never gone back into a cave, if she could help it. Especially not the sort of small, dark cave where venomous snakes piled upon one other in hissing, vicious nests.

"I hate caves," she told herself this morning—not quite quietly enough.

"Ah good, you're awake," her mother said, hearing her... and gave her a whole load of morning chores to do.

"You too, Benjamin," their mother said. "Don't go sneaking off before you're done, either!"

"Yes, Mother!" the children said, reluctant but obedient.

"We have to get that sheep," Benjamin hissed to his sister, the moment they were out of their mother's hearing range.

"Chores first," Leah replied.

"That is a chore!"

"Do you *want* Mother to find out you lost a sheep?"

Benjamin harrumphed, and hurried through his chores so

quickly and sloppily that Leah had to make him do them again, or they *would* get in trouble. Samuel joined them partway through, and Benjamin conned him into helping until Samuel's mother called him again. What with one thing and another, it was mid-afternoon before they could finally slip away.

They met at the Overlook, where they had seen the prophet. As they approached the edge, the three children stopped. From here, they could see much of the Harod Valley. The valley was a familiar sight: green with half-harvested crops. No workers were visible threshing wheat; they had already carted what grain they could up the mountain, to hide it. The messenger had ensured that.

The children hadn't heard about the messenger, but they could see for themselves what was going on: the land at the far eastern end of the valley, near the Jordan River, swarmed with the moving shapes of camels and wagons.

The first wave of intruders was arriving.

"Look how near they are!" Benjamin exclaimed excitedly. "I wonder what they look like up close."

Samuel shuddered. "I don't. Let's find that lamb and get back up here—fast."

"I don't think we should try," Leah said cautiously. "We don't know how quickly they're moving. What if there are advance scouts? What if they catch us? They'd kill us. What if they follow us back and find the caves? They'd kill *everyone*. It's not worth the risk. You'd better just tell Father about the lamb and take your punishment."

"No!" Benjamin cried. "I'm not getting in trouble just because you're scared. Besides, the Midianites are *ages* off. We have plenty of time to find the lamb. I'm not afraid!" He took off down the path at top speed.

"Benjamin!" Leah cried. "Get back here!"

He waved over his shoulder, and didn't look back. With a shrug at Leah, Samuel ran after his friend.

"Samuel, don't!" Leah yelled. "It's too dangerous! Oh! Boys!"

What was she supposed to do now? Leah scrunched her hair in her hands, trying to think. She was not about to be stupid like the boys and chase after them. She had to go back to the cave and tell Mother, and then—

And then what? What would Mother do? Only send her out after the boys—and Leah would have wasted so much time running back and forth! It was safer to go now, get the dratted lamb, and *carry* the boys to safety, if she had to.

Keeping one eye on the black stain of approaching Midianites, Leah jogged down the hill. "I have time," she told herself again and again. "Hurry, hurry, but I have time. Oh, those boys! I *am* going to tell Mother, at that!"

At least she knew where they were headed.

Leah ran so hard her gasping breaths scorched her throat dry. Despite the lightness of her step, each jog sent a jolt up her body. By the time she finally reached the spring where she'd last seen the boys, she didn't have enough breath even to grumble. She bent over a cramp, hands on hips, and looked around.

The place was deserted. There was the spring; there were the old ruins; nowhere were the boys. Where had they gone?

Lightheaded from exertion, Leah knelt and drank from the spring, trying to think. Where would the lamb have wandered off to? No, better yet—where would the boys think the lamb had wandered off to?

Leah splashed water on her face and stood, feeling refreshed. *All right*, she told herself, *I'll start by figuring out where they can't be.* To her left stood a few scattered, crumbling ruins, but the countryside beyond that was barren.

Straight ahead, the small stream tumbled downhill. The area was lined with trees and bushes and looked cool and shady. To the right, the land was open again.

Leah looked back at the shaded stream again. On a hot day like this, Benjamin and Samuel would surely go there. She thought about calling loudly for them, but remembered the Midianites. If raiders came near, they would surely see the greenery around the spring and come this way. If they were close enough, they could hear her. She'd better chase the boys quietly. She began to hurry downstream.

Where *were* those boys? Was it possible—it was almost too horrible to think—but... could they have been captured by Midianites?

Could they have been killed?

Cold shivers ran up Leah's arms, despite the heat of the day. She twitched at every sound and nearly screamed when two large *cracks* sounded near her.

What was that splashing up ahead? A camel? Oh, please let it not be a Midianite's camel!

"Die, foul Midianite!" cried Benjamin's voice. "Die!"

"I'll get him!" cried Samuel, and Leah heard another loud crack.

Protective instinct overwhelmed fear, and Leah darted forward, around the bend in the stream. There were Benjamin and Samuel—laughing?

Samuel slung his sling and sent small stone flying to *crack* against a boulder. "There's another one dead!"

"What are you doing?" Leah cried. "Are you crazy? We have to get out of here! There are *real* Midianites coming!"

"We haven't found the lamb yet," Benjamin protested. "We just got here."

"You've had enough time to start playing," Leah replied tartly. "Oh, stop it! I don't care. I'll tell our parents *I* lost the lamb. Anything! But please, please let's get back!"

Benjamin and Samuel looked at each other, uncertain. Leah's fear had finally gotten through to them. They nodded.

Samuel said, "Wait a minute," and plunked a few extra nice stones into his leather pouch. Then with sobered faces, and only one snide comment from Benjamin, they turned and followed her back upstream, toward the spring.

The trunks were too small to shelter Midianites from view. Besides, everything was so familiar—and the company so calming—that even Leah agreed when Samuel suggested taking a minute to drink from the spring.

"The lamb!" Benjamin shouted happily. "There it is!" He sprang to his feet and sprinted for the ruins, Leah and Samuel on his heels.

Sure enough, around the crumbling wall where a house had once stood, stood a lonely little lamb. Benjamin fell to his knees before it and wrapped it in a great hug. "There you are, you rascal! You almost got us in trouble!"

"Shh!" Leah shushed them, eyes wide with fear. "Listen!"

The boys crouched beside her, ears perked. They didn't have to ask what she'd heard: they recognized it immediately.

It was the sound of approaching camels and wagons.

The sound of the enemy.

"We have to hide," Leah whispered, voice harsh with fear. "We can't run—they'd see us in a second. Oh, what are we going to do?" She was wringing her hands now, just like her mother when she got worried. She'd never felt so helpless.

"The Stronghold," Samuel said.

"Samuel!" Benjamin snapped. "That's a secret!"

"What stronghold?" Leah asked. The trees—no, they were too narrow and short to hide in. Behind a rock? They'd be found in a moment. "Do you know a place? Oh, please hurry!"

"All right, all right," Benjamin said. "I guess this isn't the time for secrets. Follow me." Crawling to keep out of sight, he led them to the low, dark space under the fallen slab of rock. "In here. Come on." He squirmed in without waiting.

"In there?" Leah squeaked. "But what about snakes?"

"Who cares about snakes?" asked Samuel, and followed his friend in.

Leah wrung her hands, looking between the dark hole and over her shoulder. The sounds of camels and wagons were very close now. She heard an authoritative voice proclaim, "We'll camp here."

The voice had a Midianite accent. Leah shrank into herself.

"Search the area for spies and lingerers. Kill anyone you find."

"*Leah!*" The whisper was soft, but Leah flinched hard. What if someone overheard Benjamin? "*Leah! Get in here!*"

If Benjamin and Samuel were in there, Leah told herself, there couldn't possibly be venomous snakes.

She licked chapped lips. Her hands were trembling. She had to slap them over her mouth when the lamb behind her bleated, so she wouldn't scream.

"What was that?" the leader's voice asked.

"Dinner!" said another Midianite. "I'll get it."

Heavy footsteps stomped around the ruin. They'd round the corner in a second.

Leah pulled her hair to keep herself from thinking about what she was about to do, and dove in the dark hole. She wriggled forward at top speed. Even so, it seemed to take her ages. She was sure the Midianite must see her feet disappearing into the hole. But no voice raised the alarm, and no rough hands grabbed her ankles.

After nearly two body lengths, the crawlspace opened up into a room. Sunlight slanted in from the cracked ceiling, and there were no mole vipers to be seen.

Leah scuttled along the wall and then drew her knees up to her chest, hugging them and listening hard.

The lamb bleated. A man grunted softly as he picked it up. His footsteps beat against the dirt, retreating. A few seconds later, an appreciative cry went up as the Midianites saw their supper carried to them.

Benjamin and Samuel stared at her, their eyes round as coins and their cheeks strained and drained of color.

As, she supposed, hers must be.

CHAPTER SEVEN

No Other Gods

"I am the LORD your God; do not worship the
gods of the Amorites." (Judges 6:10)

Sunday evening came, and the Midianites spread across the
town of Ophrah like locusts.

On Mount Gilboa, the Israelites huddled in their caves,
terrified and angry and helpless. Few of them dared leave
shelter even under the dark of night. It was safer to hide than
to risk the double-edged swords of the Midianites.

For most of the villagers, the thought of the Midianites
below blocked out everything else. They could talk of nothing else, think of nothing else, prepare for nothing else.
Death was coming, and few among them believed there was
any escape save through hiding.

And then there was Gideon.

Nothing had been the same for him since he'd met the
angel. How long had it been since that morning, when he
had been alone threshing wheat? A few hours. A few hours,
and everything had changed. He felt ten years older, ten
years wiser. His eyesight had cleared.

Could the others see the difference in him? He was more

distant over his supper of fresh bread, perhaps. More distracted. But everyone was distracted, today.

Before he went to bed that night, Gideon took his habitual short walk outside, to check how things were. Above him, uncountable stars twinkled overhead. Below, in the valley, terrifyingly close, campfires glowed orange.

How many invaders sat around those fires, laughing and drinking and boasting about all the Israelites they were going to kill? A sick rock formed in Gideon's stomach as he looked down at pinpricks of flame. These people hated him, hated every Israelite. Any one of them would kill him, if they could.

As he stood and looked out, the LORD spoke to him once more. He stiffened in awe and attention, listening to the LORD's words:

"Take the second bull from your father's herd, the one seven years old. Tear down your father's altar to Baal and cut down the Asherah pole beside it. Then build a proper kind of altar to the LORD your God on the top of this height. Using the wood of the Asherah pole that you cut down, offer the second bull as a burnt offering."

Destroy the Baal altar and Asherah pole? Of course! That made perfect sense, especially after what the prophet had said. If the LORD was going to be on their side, they needed to show they were on His. It was like Joash had said: a show of solidarity.

Thoughts of his father brought Gideon to a grinding halt. Joash wouldn't like Gideon destroying the altar. He *really* wouldn't like it. And he wasn't alone: there were Ahab and the other elders too, not to mention Gideon's brothers, who went up and worshiped the Amorite gods. What would they think if they saw Gideon was going to destroy their place of worship? What would they *do?*

They wouldn't just stand by; that was for sure. Ahab had threatened to have Gideon whipped for speaking against the altar. Gideon wasn't afraid of whipping, and didn't think Ahab would petition hard for it. But Gideon had no doubt that Ahab would react much more strongly—and violently— if he knew Gideon was going to destroy the altar.

And that was at a normal time. Now, when stresses and fear were high? It would be more than mere violence. There would be blood.

Gideon shuddered and hugged himself, suddenly twice as cold as before. He told himself that he should trust in the LORD to protect him, but he was still afraid.

I'll do it now, by night, when no one can see, he told himself. *That way, I am both obeying God and keeping my family safe. But who can I trust to help me do God's work, even against Baal?*

He could trust Purah, and Purah would know which of the other servants to choose.

After checking around him to make sure no one was watching, Gideon crept over to Purah's shelter.

Purah had laid his sleeping mat beneath the overhang of an oddly shaped boulder. It was the humble shelter of a servant—and handy for Gideon.

Gideon bent down and shook the man. "Wake up, but be completely silent," he whispered.

Purah's eyes opened, startled, and he sat up.

"We have work to do," Gideon told him. "Secret work. First, I want nine more servants, men we can trust to do the LORD's work, even against Baal. No, not here. I'll tell you later; let's get the others."

Purah rose noiselessly and led his master toward the other servants. Secretly, he was excited. He had the feeling that he was about to be part of something very important, and he felt honored that Gideon had entrusted it to him.

With a quick, confident step, Purah went among each of his chosen servants in turn, shaking them and bidding them rise silently. Then he sent each recruit to wait at the edge of the sleeping area.

Gideon watched, pleased with Purah. Once all nine servants had gathered, he beckoned them follow and led them up toward the sacred place.

At the edge of it, he stopped. The blasphemous altar hulked black against the dark sky, ominous and cruel. Not far away, an Asherah pole bid men commit evil deeds and worship its idol. Gideon's neck prickled as he turned his back to it so he could face the servants. They were far enough away from the caves that no one would hear him speak, and he wanted to make sure that the servants knew what they were doing... and that they were on his side.

"Earlier today, an angel of the LORD came to me," Gideon began, and told the servants what had happened. Then he reminded them of the prophet's announcement. "The LORD spoke to me again, this evening," he said, and told them what God had commanded him to do. He finished, "The LORD will deliver us from the Midianites. He is on our side, and what have we done to thank him? We have allowed the Amorites to build an altar to Baal and raise an Asherah pole on our land! No longer. We must reclaim this sacred land. We must follow God's command: tear down the idolatrous altar and pole and build up an altar to the LORD. Once we have, I will take the seven-year-old bull from my father's herd and sacrifice it upon the altar as a burnt offering."

Gideon looked from one face to the next. He was utterly serious, but he felt at peace, too, knowing he was doing the right thing.

"If we destroy Baal's altar, the LORD will destroy the Midianites. But destroying the altar could be dangerous. My father and brothers will be angry, and the Amorite townsmen might kill us if they discover what we did.

"One man cannot do this on his own; but together, we can succeed. It's time to choose: idols of stone and wood or the LORD God, king of the universe.

"This is not a choice I will force upon you. If you are afraid, you may go back—as long as you keep your silence. So I ask you as men, as Israelites, as believers in the one true God: which of you will join me?"

Purah didn't hesitate; he was at Gideon's side almost before his master had finished speaking. Another man joined him, and another. All but one servant came over to stand by Gideon.

"I'm sorry," that man said. "I don't worship Baal, but I'm afraid. What will happen if I touch that altar?"

"Who are you afraid of?" Gideon asked him. "Of men or of Baal?"

The man shifted uncomfortably. "I'm not afraid of men," he said. "But if there is a supernatural power attached to that altar..." He took a step back, and Gideon thought he was going to run. Then the man stopped and said, mostly to himself, "What power has stone or wood? The LORD will protect me." With new decision, he stepped forward and joined the other servants.

Gideon looked at him in awe, and conviction hit him. Why hadn't he, Gideon, who had actually spoken to an angel, had courage enough to act in broad daylight? Why hadn't he trusted in God's protection?

Gideon vowed to himself that he would never make that mistake again. But for now, time was short. They had to get to work.

It was tempting to start by tearing down the old altar, but Gideon forced himself to work logically. While some servants gathered tools for destroying Baal's altar and others found new stones to build the LORD's altar, Gideon went down to the pasture where the seven-year-old bull was kept.

He stopped at the edge of the pasture for a long time, looking and listening for Midianites. The night was deep and quiet, and neither movement nor sound touched his senses. That was good, because if even he couldn't hear his servants, then neither could anyone else.

Content that he was safe, Gideon readied himself to face his a large, dangerous animal.

In the faint starlight, Gideon could just make out the bull's outline. Although it wasn't moving at present, he knew it was ever restless and alert. In a herd, the bull was the protector of the cows, which meant it guarded them against creatures prowling around at night.

Including humans.

Gideon knew he had to let the bull know who he was; sneaking up on the bull was a good way to get badly hurt. So he whistled softly, the low note he'd used to signal the bull since it had been a newborn calf.

The bull raised its head and grunted a greeting. Gideon whistled softly again, and the massive shape turned toward him and trotted over.

Gideon was ready for it. He offered it a sack of barley and, while it was eating, attached a rope to it.

It grunted again, content and placid, and followed him up the hill.

At the edge of the sacred place, Gideon tied the bull to a sturdy tree and then joined his men. Their pile of stones was complete, and they'd collected iron pry bars and axes.

"All right," Gideon said in a harsh whisper. "Let's tear

down these evil things."

This was more easily said than done: there was a reason Gideon had wanted ten servants to help him. The Baal altar was square—six feet across on each side—and three feet tall. No mortar held the stones together, because no mortar was necessary: the stones had been cut into blocks of varying sizes that fit together like puzzle pieces. The smallest of these pieces was not much bigger than a finger, but the largest took two men to lift.

The men labored for an hour, the chilly night air wicking sweat from their foreheads and muscled arms. They were no strangers to hard work, and they never paused until every stone from Baal's altar had been pried up and hurled off the sacred hilltop. Then they scuffed the dirt and stone that had been beneath the altar, so that no sign of it remained.

That left the Asherah pole. Gideon looked thoughtfully at it as his men took a brief break to drink water and quietly congratulate one another. Gideon had never seen an Asherah pole before. The altar to Baal had been erected first, and he had avoided the hilltop since then.

The pole wasn't quite what he had expected; its name deceived him. By the look of it, it was the carved trunk of a tree, set upright as though alive.

Gideon took up an axe and set to hacking the pole down. Once it had toppled, he gave his axe to his strongest servant and rested while the man hacked at the pole until only firewood remained.

"How would you like us to start the new altar, sir?" Purah asked. "By cutting the stones into blocks?"

"No," Gideon answered. "Scripture says we must not use any tools. Cutting the rock would pollute it. We'll build with uncut stones."

Purah nodded, accepting this. "Yes, sir," he said. "But

do you have other instructions? Shall we make the altar square or circular? Does 'no tools' mean we can't use mortar? And how big and wide should we make it?"

These were fair questions, and Gideon considered them carefully. Aside from a few rules—such as not using tools and not having any stairs going up the side—there was no standard way to make an altar.

Gideon reflected on how grateful he was to Grandmother Miriam for making him learn the laws and history of the Hebrews. He said, "I want the LORD's altar to look very different from Baal's, so anyone can see the difference from a glance. We'll make it round instead of square, and larger and taller."

All the men were watching him now, not just Purah. The one who had been the last to join them asked, "Does this mean you're going to be our Judge?"

Gideon blinked, astonished. "What?"

"You're replacing Baal with the LORD, and you're going to defeat the Midianites. Doesn't that make you a Judge?"

Gideon was still too astonished to respond, but the other servants began muttering in amazement and hope. A Judge! Could it be?

The Israelites had never had a king. In fact, most of the time, the loosely connected tribes barely acknowledged one another. All were bound by the Laws of Moses, but otherwise each village was ruled by its own elders. When they needed a leader, they followed the most important men—like Joash—whom they called princes. But even that was rare.

Rarest of all, however, a new leader would emerge. In times of great emergency, the LORD would choose a Judge. This Judge would decide legal cases, insist on the proper worship of God, and lead the Hebrews into victory against their enemies. The last such leader had been Judge Deborah—and that had been decades ago.

Did Gideon's servants expect him to lead Israel as Deborah had?

What a terrifying thought that was. "I never said that," he said. "I'm just doing what I was told. The LORD didn't tell me anything about raising an army. I'm just a farmer!"

"Or a 'mighty warrior,'" someone muttered.

"Sir," said Purah respectfully, "the angel told you that you were going to strike down the Midianites. How could you do that without an army?"

Gideon wasn't ready to think about that yet. So he said gruffly, "Let's just build this altar," and walked over to the pile of fresh stones.

Constructing the altar took hours. They put the largest, heaviest stones on the bottom, and worked up from that strong foundation. For mortar, they used a combination of small rocks and mud, filling the cracks and smoothing over the surface. None of them had built an altar before, but all had worked on houses, and this wasn't much different.

When the altar was tall enough, they laid flat stones over the edges. The very center of the altar, they had left hollow. In this way, they could build a fire in the middle of the altar to burn the meat laid across the top.

At least, that was how Gideon had always seen the priests do it.

He'd expected himself to be nervous at this point, putting himself in the place of a priest, as if he were doing something wrong. But he wasn't nervous. If God Himself had ordered him to do this, it couldn't be wrong—the only wrong thing would be not offering the sacrifice correctly and reverently.

Speaking of which, his men could use another breather. "Drink some water," he told them, "and prepare yourselves as I build the fire. Then we will make a proper sacrifice to the Lord and reclaim this sacred hillside in His name."

A quiet cheer rose up among the servants, their excitement driving away the burning of their muscles and the fatigue of half-a-night's labor on little sleep. They gathered before the altar as Gideon took the wood pieces of Asherah pole, set them inside the altar, and started the fire.

Without having to be asked, Purah brought him the bull. Gideon laid both his hands ritualistically on the bull's head, to demonstrate that the bull was a gift from him, personally, to the Lord. He blessed the animal for sacrifice to God, and then drew his knife and swiftly killed it.

God commanded that no Hebrew drink an animal's blood, because the life of every sort of animal is in its blood. Since the bull's life was exactly what Gideon was giving the Lord, he collected some of the bull's blood in a bowl and splashed it on the altar in the traditional way: some on top, some around the stone sides, and the rest around the base.

Next, Gideon began cutting up the bull's body and washing every bit of it, even the hooves. The servants, who knew what to expect, made sure they brought him everything he needed for this, including plenty of water. Preparing the bull was a long process, and it was meant to be. Every part of it was service to the Lord.

"Now," Gideon said, "we will make a burnt offering, as God commanded." His servants helped him lift the pieces of bull onto the altar, over the blazing fire.

Since this was a burnt offering, instead of a different type of sacrifice, Gideon would burn every bit of the bull to ashes. This was the same kind of sacrifice Noah had made after the flood was over: a total sacrifice, with nothing held back.

A seven-year-old grown bull took a long time to burn to ashes, even cut into chunks as this one was—and the night had already been long. Though the men worked steadily, keeping the fire blazing hot, the sky was lightening as the last of the sacrifice fell to ash.

Only then did Gideon lead his men back to the caves. Keeping a sharp eye out for early risers, they crept back to bed and collapsed into exhausted sleep.

CHAPTER EIGHT

Trapped

The hours passed with agonizing slowness. If not for the sun's progress down into evening and then night, Leah wouldn't have believed time was passing at all.

The children didn't dare talk above the slightest breath, and then only sparingly. They could hear the Midianites so clearly, they knew the raiders would also be able to hear them.

To pass the hours, they drank a little from Leah's skin bag and shared a piece of bread from Samuel's pouch, and they waited and listened. At one point, Samuel briefly fell asleep.

A lot of what the Midianites said was ordinary, like Hebrews might have said about putting up camp and preparing supper and scouting. But they said other things, too. Uglier things. And the way they said them was different.

The children shivered and covered their ears, but they could not block out the voices. And slowly, they began to recognize the different voices and identify the speakers by name.

"Seriously," one man complained. "Why do we have to stay in this—this—this—achoo! Ugh."

"Camp? Because we're watching, obviously. Gross, Ebdor, wipe your nose. Do you have to sneeze all the time?"

"It's this—this—this—"

"Cover your face! Of all people to get stuck on guard duty with, why did I have to get the sneezer?"

"It's not my fault, Gobel! It's not like I want to—to—to—"

"Don't you do it!"

Ebdor sneezed noisily.

Hay fever, Leah thought. *Serves you right for coming where you aren't welcome!*

"Is that lamb done yet?" Gobel asked. "Give me a chunk. Ah, it's good to eat lamb again."

"We must have killed fifty sheep today," Ebdor answered with a laugh. "The dogs will eat well tonight."

"I know something else I'd like to feed to the dogs."

"If we find those Hebrews tomorrow and leave the next day, it won't be—achoo!—soon enough for me. Ugh, this valley. How can anyone stand to live here?"

Gobel didn't sound concerned. He was too busy chewing as he spoke. "Better get used to it, because Commander Oreb plans to stay here a nice long time. Let the main horde head west to the sea when it gets here; we already have everything we need. Wheat and barley now, figs in June. And there are plenty more sheep where this one came from."

"But my *nose!*"

"Stop sneezing, and it won't bother you. How are you going to kill Hebrews if you're sneezing all the time?"

"I could kill Hebrews with my eyes shut and one hand tied behind my back. Stupid pigs."

"More like stupid flies: pests, and not even good to eat."

Ebdor broke into a hoarse laugh, interspersed with sneezes. Leah clenched her fists and tried not to listen to the men describing the way they'd kill any Hebrews they found. It was too awful.

"And if we don't find them," Gobel said gleefully, "we'll just destroy everything and let 'em starve."

A poke tickled Leah's side, and she jerked, then glared at Benjamin.

"Leah!" he hissed.

Leah put her finger to her lips.

"Leah, are you listening to this? These guys aren't part of the main invasion—they came before the rest. That means that if we can get away from here, we're safe. There can't be that many of them."

"Quiet," Leah cautioned in a voiceless whisper. "They'll hear you!"

Benjamin, as usual, ignored her. "We'll go when it's full dark except for the crescent moon."

Samuel shoved his head in close to theirs. "They'd catch us!" he said nervously.

"No, they won't," said Benjamin. "And if they do, at least we'll have a quick death. We'll starve if we stay here."

Leah had to admit that he had a point. "But how can we get away?" she asked. "They'd see us!"

"Did you hear that?" Ebdor asked suddenly, interrupting his own string of complaints. Inside the Stronghold, the children froze. "What was that?"

"Hmm?" mumbled Gobel through yet another mouthful of food.

"I heard a sound on the breeze, like the whispering of children." His feet scuffed the dirt as he stood.

"Oh, sit down, you fool. It's your imagination."

"It's *not* my imagination. This place is haunted!"

"Don't be stupid," said Gobel, but he sounded worried. "Wait, where are you going? Don't leave me alone! Come back!"

Hardly believing their luck, the children listened as the

two guards crunched away. They waited, but there was no sound of footsteps returning.

"Ghosts?" Samuel said, and had to press his hands to his mouth to suppress his giggles. His laughter was catching, and soon all three children were rocking with suppressed hilarity.

Leah recovered herself first. "We'd better sneak away now, before someone comes out," she said.

"But it's not fully dark yet!"

"No, but we might not get a better chance. Oh, I wish we knew if there are other guards out there."

"I'm not afraid to look," Benjamin whispered, and began squirming out through the hole before the others could respond.

"I'm the eldest," Leah offered weakly, secretly glad not to have to go first. Besides, she knew Benjamin: when he wasn't doing something silly, he was by far the sneakiest of them all.

If she had asked him, Benjamin would have agreed with her. He had played battle games throughout these ruins hundreds of times. He knew every hiding place, every climbing hold, and every spy crack. He could tiptoe over the rubble without a sound, one shadow among many.

Tonight wasn't a game—his heart thumped with excitement and fear—but he moved with habitual grace and stealth.

Squirrel-like, Benjamin scuttled up an old wall, fingers expertly clutching invisible handholds in ancient stone. Head cocked for the slightest suspicious noise, he slid onto his stomach, flat atop the wall, and peered around.

A short distance off to the north, near the spring, campfires lit the sleeping forms of dozens of men. The campfires stretched down to the east and southeast, which was the direction the Midianites had come from. Dozens more—no, hundreds!—camped by the eastern side of Mount Gilboa.

Exhausted from their long march and from the destruction they had wrought, most of the Midianites were asleep or drunk with wine. But the guards were awake and alert, ready to capture and kill any sheep–or Israelites—they could catch. Not even the cleverest three children could get past them without being seen; it was impossible.

Benjamin memorized the positions of the fires, then prepared to climb back down. As he did, he happened to glance directly below him—and nearly dropped off.

Three men slept on the ground outside the wall, six feet below him, their razor-sharp swords glinting in the starlight. If any one of them happened to awake and look up, he couldn't avoid seeing Benjamin.

Very, very quietly, Benjamin slithered back down his side of the wall and crept to the opposite end of the ruin, to see what lay in that direction.

From here, he could look at the land west of him—in the direction of his home. Not the cave in the hills; his real home.

There were fewer campfires in this direction, and only a few small groups of men. This briefly puzzled Benjamin. He'd have assumed that they'd want to get close to the village so they could more easily go after the Hebrews they thought living within.

Then the answer came to him, and he trembled with sudden fear.

The Midianites didn't care about the village, because they knew there weren't any people there. They cared about Mount Gilboa.

They knew, or suspected, where the Hebrews had hidden.

Benjamin's parents thought they were safe in the caves. But what they really were was trapped. Tomorrow, or the day after, or when the other Midianites arrived—it didn't matter when it happened. It was just a matter of time before the Midianites advanced and killed them all.

There could be no more hiding.

Benjamin felt sick. His lingering confidence vanished like a puff of smoke. No, these weren't the Midianites they'd been afraid of for so many years—those were yet to come. And when they did...

He had to tell someone, had to get to the leaders. But, with a sick feeling, Benjamin realized how impossible that was. If he went back, he'd only be trapped with the rest—and he'd be trapping Samuel and Leah along with him. The only way to keep them alive was to run far and fast in the opposite direction.

Would they agree? He suspected they wouldn't; they'd want to go back to the leaders. They still believed the adults could keep them safe. So had he, until ten seconds ago.

He had to keep the truth of the situation to himself, no matter how frightened he was.

Benjamin licked his lips and jumped down to the ground. He stumbled on the rocks, nearly turning his ankle, and froze.

"What was that?" an enemy voice asked. It sounded more sleepy than worried.

"Your imagination," muttered another voice. "Shut up and go back to sleep."

Benjamin hardly dared breathe. His heart sounded impossibly loud in his ears. But the man apparently decided he had imagined or dreamed the noise, and soon Benjamin could hear only the steady rise and fall of sleep.

Tense and sweating, Benjamin crept back to the tunnel and squirmed in.

When he spoke, his voice was so quiet that Leah and Samuel had to lean in close to hear. "We can make it," he breathed. "Not to the hills but into the valley. They don't care about our houses; we can hide in there and then escape."

"Are you *sure*?" Leah asked.

"Sure I'm sure! You coming or not? Follow me exactly and don't make a sound, and you'll be fine!"

Wishing he was as confident as he sounded, Benjamin led Samuel and Leah out into the night. The thin sliver of moon gave little light, but stars pricked the sky like drops of liquid silver. Together, the three children stood among the broken pillars and fallen rubble of the ancient building. They were alone in here.

Outside, their enemies were quiet. The night's silence was broken only by the occasional shuffling of animal hooves and the small talk of guards. The children didn't realize it, but this wasn't a real army with trained sentries posted all around—it was a mob of desert warriors, undisciplined, unruly, and unfriendly to itself as well as to others. The warriors had only come together so they could invade the valley with force. They didn't know or trust one another, and half of the guards were asleep or drunk.

Benjamin crooked his finger at his sister and friend, and then led them on the path he'd scouted out. He scaled the unguarded wall and slithered down the other side. Once the other two joined him, he set off at a light jog toward the village.

Some instinct alerted him just in time, and Benjamin fell to his stomach. Leah and Samuel dove down on either side of him, pulses racing. As Samuel turned his head to ask his friend what the matter was, a sentry's soft feet padded across the grass not twenty feet in front of them.

They had been lucky; he was looking in a different direction and hadn't seen them.

They clutched at the ground, unmoving, not daring even to slink backward.

The sentry turned, and they saw another join him and speak in low voices. Benjamin could only hear fragments—

"Israelites from—"

"—try to return—"

"—village—"

He listened hard and managed to piece together what was going on. A group of Midianites had surrounded Ophrah in the hope that some Israelites might try to sneak back and recover a portion of what had been left behind.

If the children went that way, they'd be walking into a trap.

It seemed to take ages for the patrollers to turn and go on their way, and even then Benjamin hardly dared shift enough to turn his head and breathe into first Leah's ear and then Samuel's, "We have to go back."

Their eyes shone round and white, and their heads nodded. Crawling on their bellies like worms, they inched back toward the Stronghold to hole up, hungry and frightened, and wait for daylight.

CHAPTER NINE

Jerub-Baal

"They asked each other, 'Who did this?'"
(Judges 6:29)

The Israelites hadn't missed the way the Midianites had camped up against the base of Mount Gilboa—or what it meant for their future. The current force might be too small to attack them on their own turf, but the main horde would be here soon—in a day or two—and then it would only be a matter of time.

Gideon wasn't the only one who had spent a sleepless night. Several of the others had grouped up to speak in low, worried voices about what they could do next. If there was anything they could do.

By the time Gideon and his servants were collapsing, exhausted from their sleepless night, at least one group had come to a decision. Ahab and his cronies gathered up their fellow Amorites and any Israelites who worshiped Baal for one final, desperate march up to the sacred hilltop.

"The Midianites have found us," Ahab announced. "That's why they camped there. So far, only scattered raiding parties have arrived, but they're growing bolder. They might not even wait for the main Midianite force to arrive before they attack us. Regardless, one way or another, they plan to kill us.

"Our forces are small, too small and weak to fight back with any hope of victory. We know we cannot survive on our own, so we have only one recourse: we must seek divine assistance. We must get Baal on our side."

"But what more can we do?" Joash wondered. "We make many sacrifices to Baal. We made one the day before last! We've done all we can do to make him help us."

"We think we have, but how can we be sure?" asked another man, one of Ahab's cronies. "We need to be absolutely sure."

"And there is a way to be sure," Ahab said. "We offer Baal something huge—a sacrifice so great that he'll have no choice but to help us. Now, what's the biggest sacrifice we could make?"

"That's easy," said a rough-faced woman whose youngest child was six years old. "Infant sacrifice."

"She has a point," said another woman. "What could be more valuable to Baal than sacrificing a baby?"

"I agree," said Ahab, who had planned this whole conversation for the benefit of the newcomers. "Human sacrifice is powerful, and the sacrifice of the innocent most powerful still. In fact, the more innocent the better—which means we should choose an Israelite baby. Yes, that would please Baal greatly."

"Human sacrifice!" cried Joash, horrified. "Madness! Murder! I won't permit it."

Ahab smiled thinly. "You won't have a choice."

Joash looked around at the hard, leering faces, and fear tinged his anger. He said, almost pleading, "Is this the thanks I get for allowing you to build an altar on my land? Madness and murder?"

"Oh, come on," Ahab said, rolling his eyes. "You knew what kind of god Baal was when you agreed to the altar. Of course human sacrifice is necessary. Anyway, what is one death compared to the deaths of every man, woman, and child on this mountain?

"You know as much as any of us that we must have Baal's help. And he will help us, if we do this one thing. Now isn't the time for squeamishness or cowardice. Be a man, Joash. Join us and do what's right."

Joash was shaking his head and backing away. "This is wrong," he said. "Wrong."

"Wrong to worship Baal as he demands? That's not what you've said before. Be consistent."

Joash pressed his palms to his temples. How his head ached! "Our Lord, the God of Israel, hates human sacrifice," he said. He suddenly saw Baal-worship for what it was. How could he ever have gone along with it?

Because his friends had. Because it was easy. Because he hadn't stopped to *think*.

"What nonsense," Ahab snapped. "You don't care what the LORD thinks, or you wouldn't be worshiping Baal. Besides, every god demands human sacrifice sometimes. Stop trying to be special. You hypocrite."

Joash bowed his head, having trouble understanding what was going on. These men and women were his neighbors, and he'd thought them his friends. He'd worked alongside them, laughed alongside them. He respected them; they honored him as the owner of the altar. Would they really do something terrible?

And yet he knew, without a fragment of doubt, that what they wanted to do was wrong. Even if they planned to choose one of their own infants, it would be wrong.

"If Ahab told you to steal something, would you do it?"

Gideon had asked him that, and he'd let Ahab dismiss the young man in offended anger. Now, his son's words came back to haunt him.

Joash backed away another step, shaking his head, and turned to leave. How many times had he broken the commandments to only worship the Lord, shun idols, and keep the Sabbath? He'd sinned against the Lord so many times, he'd thought he'd forgotten how to say no.

But he had found his sticking point—and in finding it, he felt sick to remember his other sins.

Ahab tilted his head, looking at Joash in confusion. He'd been so sure of winning, he could hardly believe Joash wasn't playing along. "Aren't you coming?"

"No." Joash didn't explain. He simply turned his back on the Amorites and walked away.

It was time to have another chat with Gideon.

He heard, behind him, the Amorites exclaiming about his betrayal and then shrugging it off. He wasn't so important to them after all.

He had a hard time not hating himself.

Ahab had implied that a real man would sacrifice a baby to Baal, but Joash suspected that what a real man would actually do was destroy the altar to Baal. *Am I a coward?* he wondered. But he didn't stop walking. He knew he couldn't stop Ahab's followers alone, and that he needed to protect his own family.

Dismissing Joash's negative reaction from his mind, Ahab directed his fellow Amorites to follow him up to the sacred hilltop. "Gather firewood as we go," he said. "We will make the initial preparations. Once they are complete, we can decide on an infant to sacrifice. We won't give the Israelites time to object."

The other Amorites cheered and followed him up. Ahab wondered whose baby he should sacrifice. He should pick one from the family he hated the most. Yes, that was an excellent idea.

Ahab became so wrapped up in his schemes that they were nearly at the top of the hilltop before his nostrils registered the familiar scents of a burnt offering: smoke, charred meat, blood. Had someone already begun sacrificing to Baal without them? *I bet it was Joash, the old hypocrite*, Ahab thought, chuckling to himself.

Then he remembered the approaching Midianites and sobered. Despite what Joash probably thought of him—and despite his own comforting thoughts of revenge—part of Ahab was slightly squeamish about human sacrifice.

That's the point, he told himself. *That's what makes* this *sacrifice so great. It's tough to make.*

He glanced over his shoulder, down the mountain. The many trees blocked the Midianites from seeing the Israelites, but they wouldn't block out the smoke from the sacrifice.

Well, so be it. The Midianites clearly already knew where they were. His hope for survival was no longer in secrecy but in Baal.

Ahab redoubled his stride, and they crested the sacred hilltop.

Something was wrong.

Ahab skittered to a stop, eyes bulging. The altar—that wasn't Baal's altar! It was bigger and round and made with mortar and uncut stones. And—and where was the Asherah pole?

"Who did this?" the Amorites asked one another. "Who did this?"

Who had been sacrificing to this new god?

80

Or... *was* it a new god?

Anger flamed hot between Ahab's ears as he realized what was going on. Betrayed! The Israelites had betrayed them all by tearing down Baal's altar and raising one to their Lord!

Ahab looked down at his hands, clenching them. If that's how it was going to be, then let this altar be the cause of murder. "I'm going to find out who did this," he growled to the other Amorites, "and I'm going to kill him with my own hands. Let *his* burnt body please Baal!"

As Ahab had fumed, the other Amorites had been coming to the same conclusions. Hearing him, they rallied and cheered, their bloodlust heightened by fear and thoughts of revenge.

"To the Israelite caves!" Ahab cried. "Question those worms until you find out who tore down Baal's altar and built that abomination in its place. Raise the cry, and don't let him escape. Let's go!"

With a yell, he charged down the hill, his horde flooding after him. Soon, the younger Amorites overtook him, sending small cascades of dirt and pebbles down the mountain before them. They grabbed the Israelites who were awake and roughly shook those who weren't. "Who did it?" they demanded. "Tell us, or we'll hurt you. Who destroyed Baal's altar and built a new one to the Lord?"

"I don't know!" claimed the frightened Israelites.

"But I'd like to congratulate him!" added the bravest among them.

"But that's terrible!" added those who had taken on Amorite ways.

Not all the Amorites were rough in their interrogations. Despite his anger, Ahab investigated methodically and carefully. He asked everyone again and again, "Who did it, who did it?" Almost everyone said they didn't know, including the Amorites they questioned. It was impossible to know who was lying and who was telling the truth, but at last, they had their answer:

"Gideon son of Joash did it."

When Ahab heard those words, he clenched his fists and roared, forehead throbbing purple. "Gideon did it!" he cried. "Gideon did it! Gideon ruined our only chance of survival! Gideon destroyed Baal's altar! Gideon did it!"

Others took up the shout until most of the villagers joined Ahab in a frenzy. Gone were the peaceable neighbors; in their place screamed a furious mob. They crashed between trees and stormed up to the very entrance of Gideon's cave...

And stopped.

There was Joash, waiting. Infuriated though the villagers were, Joash still commanded their respect. They were willing to listen to him, though they were on edge, frightened and angry.

Ahab elbowed his way to the front of the mob. "Bring out your son," he snarled at Joash. "He must die, because he has broken down Baal's altar and cut down the Asherah pole beside it."

Joash stayed calm before them, leaning on his staff. He did not look surprised or upset, because he wasn't. When he had left the Amorites in disgust and come to Gideon's cave, he had found his son collapsed on a sleeping mat, unwashed, having not even taken off his sandals. When he had touched his son's shoulder, Gideon had awoken, and there had been something in his eyes—a brightness.

"You'll be angry with me, Father," he'd told Joash, "but I won't hide from you what I've done." Then he'd sat himself comfortably cross-legged, and began talking about angels and divine commands and seven-year-old bulls.

Joash had listened, tears glistening in his eyes. Tears for

himself, that he had failed before the LORD—and tears of pride in his son.

"I will protect you from them when they come," he'd promised. "Be ready."

And now they'd come, and Joash was fulfilling his promise. He considered Ahab and the crowd. When his calm had steadied them, and he could see that he had their full attention, he spoke in his most reasonable, authoritative voice—one pitched to appeal to friends and enemies alike. "Are you going to plead Baal's cause?" he asked, disbelief in his voice. "Are you trying to *save* him?" He barked out a laugh. "Whoever fights for him shall be put to death by morning! If Baal really is a god," he added, a touch sarcastic, as if this were the most ridiculous thing in the world, "he can defend himself when someone breaks down his altar."

Amorites and Israelites alike looked at one another. They liked and respected Joash… and he had an awfully good point.

"If Baal can't protect himself, how can he protect us?" someone wondered.

"Will we really die if we fight for him?"

"If the LORD's altar has replaced Baal's, the LORD must be stronger."

"We don't have time to build a new altar for Baal, especially now we've displeased him. No sacrifice would be enough. We have to rely on the LORD."

"Finally," said Grandmother Miriam, who had emerged from her cave to see what was going on, "the evil altar to the false god has been destroyed. The LORD's will be done."

Several faithful Israelites nearby overheard her and immediately put in their voices to agree. Arguments broke out, then shut up a second later.

Gideon had emerged.

He climbed out the mouth of the cave and stood beside his father, tall, strong, and confident. The light Joash had seen in his son was now seen by all. "You're right," he said, and he hardly had to raise his voice for everyone to hear him. "I tore down Baal's altar, and I'm not afraid of him. If Baal's angry, let him come after me. The LORD commanded me to do what I have done. Is there anyone here who would fight me over that—who would fight Him?"

The Amorites shrank from him. Many looked to Ahab for guidance, but Ahab shrank away with the rest of them. He had never seen Gideon looking like this—so powerful... and he was mindful of the mood of the crowd. Ahab had riled them up, gotten them on his side, but he was no longer so sure of his support. If he tried to fight them, there would be bloodshed... and it might be *his* blood that was shed.

"Oh, let Baal deal with him," he said in disgust. "This isn't our problem."

Someone laughed. "What do you think about that, Jerub-Baal? You afraid?"

"No," said Gideon, smiling, "because the LORD is on my side."

"Jerub-Baal," Ahab said. "Yes, let that be your name. For better or worse."

"For better," Joash said firmly, more proud than ever of his son. There was a long tradition, among Hebrews, that if something so great happened that it changed a person, that person would receive a new name. Abraham's wife Sarai had been renamed Sarah, and Jacob had become Israel. Joash could see the change and growth in his son, and Jerub-Baal was a fitting new name, for it meant "Let Baal deal with him." No one who heard that name could doubt that Gideon was a man with the power to break down Baal's altar without retribution.

"The Midianites are camped below," Jerub-Baal told the villagers, "but the LORD will protect us." He spoke to them for a long time, first reminding them of what the prophet had said and then telling them of the angel and God's commands. He finished by saying, "We must worship the LORD and obey all of His commandments if we want Him to save us from the Midianites. I tore down Baal's altar. Now, you must tear Baal out of your hearts."

That morning, the Israelites began to speak of Jerub-Baal as their Judge.

CHAPTER TEN

In the Valley

"They came up with their livestock and their tents like swarms of locusts." (Judges 6:5)

Commander Zeeb looked over the Harod Valley with eyes that glinted golden in the sunlight. Those eyes were what had gotten him his name, which meant "wolf."

It was a fitting name, and Zeeb rejoiced in it. Wolves were fierce predators that traveled in packs and were willing to attack animals far larger than themselves. A boy with rocks might scare off one lion, but not a pack of wolves.

Like his namesake, Zeeb lived for the joy of hunting, tracking, chasing, and killing. Nothing frightened him. He dressed simply in a white tunic, his only jewelry gold earrings and pendants. He didn't want anything to hamper him as he fought. The spoils of his kills, he kept on his camel, which carried enough gold to feed a man for a lifetime.

Now, eyes gleaming from recent violence, Zeeb returned to his masters—the Midianite kings. He made his camel kneel and then leapt off to bow in the usual manner: legs folded under him and face to the ground. Despite his humble attitude, however, nothing could disguise the ferocity of his movements. That was why King Zalmunna liked him so much… and why King Zebah always felt so uncomfortable around him.

"Rise and join us," Zalmunna offered.

Zeeb the Wolf rose and went to sit with them. A servant handed him a wineskin, which he drank from greedily. Murder was thirsty work.

"What do you have to report?" Zebah asked. He lolled on cushions his servants had arranged for him. He was shorter and fatter than King Zalmunna, but like him, he was dressed in purple robes. The eye-catching reddish-purple dye had been painstakingly produced from shellfish in the Mediterranean Sea and was so expensive that only kings could afford it. The material alone was probably worth more than the gold rings, pendants, and earrings weighing down the kings, but even that represented only a tiny fraction of their wealth.

Like Zeeb—like all Midianites—the kings carried their wealth on their camels and donkeys. Surrounding the camels' necks and dangling down were golden ornaments shaped like drops of water; and from each of these hung seven smaller, drop-shaped pieces of gold. Engraved on them were little crescent moons. Their donkeys carried yet more gold—all the kings owned, in fact, because the Midianites were nomads. It made no sense to bury their gold when they were constantly moving around.

His thirst quenched, Zeeb made his report: "Most of our men have entered the Harod Valley. The Amalekites should be joining us soon—in fact, some rode in with our troops."

"Good," said Zalmunna, nodding, gold ornaments swaying. "What about Oreb?"

"He spent the night south of here, not far from a spring, but it proved unsuitable for our larger force. I ordered him to tighten up on discipline. We don't want his troops scattered too near the mountain, where they'll be vulnerable." Commander Zeeb looked around, frowning. "He said he'd be right behind me—ah. There he is now."

Commander Oreb had just come into view, mounted on his camel. Like Zeeb, he was named after an animal—in his case, a raven. The Israelites considered ravens unclean, because they ate carrion. In addition to rotting dead animals, ravens ate fruit, seeds, small birds, and baby animals— basically, anything that couldn't fight back. Not unlike Oreb.

Zeeb looked scornfully at his fellow commander. Oreb's hair was black and shiny as a raven's feathers, and his nose was sharp as a beak. Zeeb didn't approve of Oreb, who took little pleasure in the hunt. All Oreb cared about was the shiny loot he could carry off after a kill.

King Zebah nodded to the newly arrived commander. Oreb didn't make him uncomfortable like Zeeb, and they shared a passion for loot. "Have you found any good treasure?" he asked the commander. "Sit, eat."

Oreb the Raven reached for the fruit bowl with a filthy hand. Blood and dirt stained his white tunic, not that he cared. "Not as much as I would have liked, but I did my best for you, Excellency. I killed the Israelites who were guarding it, but there weren't many around; most of them had run off to hide before we got there."

King Zalmunna made a disgusted noise and shook his head. "It's past time we dealt with those vermin. As soon as our men are gathered, we'll form an organized attack and wipe them from the face of the earth."

King Zebah shook his head. "That sounds like far too much effort—and it's not as though the Israelites can hurt us. Why not just raid the empty villages and carry off everything we find? As long as the Israelites stay alive, they'll produce an endless supply of loot."

Zeeb the Wolf licked his lips. "Or we could break into smaller packs. That way, we could move all through the Jezreel Valley, spreading out in every direction. If we stay ahead of the Amalekites, we can pick and choose what we want. Let them have our leftovers."

"Are you crazy?" Oreb the Raven said angrily. "Move on, while there's still so much to loot here? I could raid this valley all summer and not be done with it. I don't want to leave a grain of wheat to the Amalekites."

King Zalmunna listened to the argument for several minutes before raising his hand. He was willing to hear them out, but he had the final say. "We will gather as one army with the Amalekites," he said. "I want to destroy the Israelites; they're too dangerous. Separate, we might not be strong enough, if they resist. But together, I defy them or their God to hurt us."

CHAPTER ELEVEN

Call to Arms

"Now all the Midianites, Amalekites and other
eastern peoples joined forces and crossed over
the Jordan and camped in the Valley of Jezreel."
(Judges 6:33)

"Judge Gideon! Jerub-Baal!" the messenger threw himself off
his horse at Gideon's feet. "It's the main force! They're arriving in the valley!"

"How do you know that name?" Gideon asked in aston-
ishment. Not even a day had passed since the villagers had
confronted him and called him Jerub-Baal, "Let Baal deal with
him." In fact, many villagers were still with him here at the
meeting place, milling around and talking. Now, they
stopped to listen to what the messenger had to say.

The messenger lifted his head. "News spreads quickly,
sir. I have heard of the LORD's angel coming to you, and of
the destruction of Baal's altar." He looked to Gideon. "Am I
wrong? Are you not the mighty warrior who will save us
from the Midianites?"

"The LORD will save us," Gideon said. "But you are right
that I now lead our people as Judge." How strange it felt,

saying that! But it felt right, too. "Tell me everything you know; I need all your information. How many invaders are there? What weapons do they have? How far up the valley are they, and how quickly are they moving?"

"They fill the valley and cover the fields," the young man answered, putting his hands together and then spreading them wide. "Like a swarm of locusts they've come, destroying everything in their way. They're riding camels, leading pack camels and donkeys, and bringing enough tents for a city."

The messenger looked toward the valley below, his home. "We estimate they have 130,000 men. They're halfway into the Harod Valley and more are coming all the time." His words were bleak, but not hopeless, and he looked at Gideon with trusting eyes.

Gideon was stunned. "This is more than ever before. Are they all Midianites?"

The young man shook his head. "Midianites, yes, but also Amalekites and other tribes from the eastern desert."

Gideon sat down hard on a nearby rock, trying to think. A hundred thirty thousand men! That was far, far more than he could gather. Even if he had the numbers, he wasn't sure he could beat the Midianites and Amalekites in a straight fight, because the nomads were fierce fighters and mounted on camels. How could men on foot hope to beat them?

"Only God could win against such invaders," he said.

It was the right thing to say. He stood again and shouted it so that everyone could hear: "Only the LORD can win against such invaders—and the LORD is on our side!"

As Gideon spoke, the Spirit of the LORD came upon him, and he knew what he had to do. He took up a trumpet and blew it again and again, summoning his fellow Abiezrites to him. The whole village came flooding in, so all could hear him. The trumpet blow was the ancient call to battle.

Gideon spread his arms wide. "We will fight our enemies, and our God will save us!" he announced. "Come together, all Abiezrites! Come to the LORD's victory! Messengers, come forward! Run throughout Manasseh and summon every fighting man! Call the other tribes as well—call Asher, Zebulun, and Naphtali. Bring them to join us in the battle by Wednesday night. Together, united, with the LORD's help, we will defeat our enemies!"

As he spoke, the Abiezrites' excitement grew into feverish delight. Forgetting their danger, forgetting everything but hope and trust, they cheered. When Gideon dismissed them, they scattered to the winds to prepare, faces aglow with hope and faith.

Only one man hung back, sour and hateful, until the others had left Gideon and Joash alone. This was Judah, Gideon's eldest brother.

Tall and broad-shouldered, with the proud posture of a king, Judah looked very similar to his youngest brother. On the inside, however, the two men were very different.

Several years ago, when the Amorites asked their father to let them build an altar to Baal on his land, Gideon had argued strongly against it. Judah, however, had been delighted. He bragged that this showed how important his family's land was! He often bragged about his family's close ties to Baal, as if Baal were their personal friend.

Like his father, Judah had begun worshiping Baal. But he had gone even further than Joash in joining the Amorites, and he had done many evil things. He even hoped to someday take part in an infant sacrifice.

Gideon's steadfast devotion to the LORD infuriated and disgusted him. If Judah had bothered to examine himself to discover just why he was so against Gideon following God's commands, he might have discovered the truth. He might have discovered that Gideon's obedience made him feel guilty—that deep down, he knew that Gideon was doing right and he was doing wrong.

But Judah was not prone to self-examination or ever admitting fault. He preferred to blame other people for his faults. When possible, he liked to make people do what he wanted; when not possible, he liked to hate them.

On this occasion, Judah sneered full force at his youngest brother. A Midianite could not have hated the new Judge more. "What do you think you're doing?" Judah asked. "Look at you, saying you talked to an angel. Don't you know the difference between reality and fantasy? Either you dreamed the angel or—more likely—you made him up entirely. Pathetic, the things some people will do to make themselves feel important."

"Hello, Judah," Gideon said, fighting to keep his temper. No good could come of arguing with his brother; he'd learned that while they were still children.

Judah saw Gideon's self-control and determined to break through it. He crossed the remaining distance and shouted in the Judge's face, "You had no right to tear down our altar, you self-absorbed, self-centered little liar! Stop making yourself out to be some sort of prophet when everyone really knows you're a nobody, the youngest son of a farmer—and a traitor to our people!"

"Now wait, boys," Joash interrupted. Although his sons were adults, he couldn't help but think of them as children. "Let's talk this over."

Judah spat at Gideon's feet. "You hide behind your father's cloak, boy. Our brothers and all our family are on my side. This evening, we're going to help the Amorites rebuild Baal's altar, and we're going to make such a sacrifice at it that nobody will *ever* forget. We will have saved our people. *Us.* Because when we go into battle, it'll be under Baal's protection."

"No, you mustn't!" Gideon cried. "If you do, you'll be killed!"

"Are *you* threatening *me?*"

"I'm warning you!"

"Enough, boys. Enough." Joash pushed between them, and they stepped back instinctively. "Judah, you'll have enemies enough to fight soon. Leave your brother in peace."

"Gideon has made himself my enemy."

"Judah," said Gideon, "don't do this thing. Don't make yourself God's enemy."

Judah's eyes flamed. "You think you have power," he said. "Well, you don't. I do." He spun on his heel and strode off, to go fume at his wife and friends... and to think of how he could strike back at his brother.

Joash watched his eldest son sadly. Until now, they had been on such good terms—but of course, he reflected, until now, Joash had been joining Judah in the Amorites' evil. It was time he stood with his youngest son, the one doing God's work.

But oh, it hurt to see Judah so angry at him.

A thump turned Joash's attention back to Gideon. The young man had collapsed heavily onto a boulder, unhappiness weighing his youthful face down into deep folds.

Joash put his hand on his son's shoulder. "He'll come around," he said, insufficiently. "He loves you, deep down. As you love him."

"I know," Gideon said miserably. "He's afraid—we all are. But it isn't that, or not only that." He scrubbed his face with hands, his shoulders quivering.

Joash sat next to his son, one arm around him, and waited.

"What if he's right, Father?" Gideon burst out, slamming his fists on his knees. "What if I did dream it? What if I am a fool?"

"You didn't dream it."

"No, you're right. I know I didn't. But—but God didn't exactly *promise* me we'd win. I mean, it sounded like He was promising me that—I thought He was promising that—but now I'm not sure…. What if I missed something important? What if I did something wrong? What if he changed his mind? I just need to *know*. If God isn't going to win this battle for us, we'll all die. Horribly. We *can't* do this by ourselves, even with the other tribes helping. If I'm wrong, I could be leading every man in our valley to his death—and every woman and child into slavery or worse!"

Joash listened patiently and then considered the matter. He thought back to Scripture, to the Judges of the past. Then he stood and made Gideon stand and face him. "You've spoken with the LORD before," he told his son, "and He gave you a sign that the angel was really His. Why don't you speak with Him again? Ask Him for a sign that He will save us."

Gideon stared at his father for a long moment, and then laughed and flung his arms around him in a tight hug. "You are wise, Father," he said.

Joash slapped him on the back and kissed his forehead. "You're a good boy, Gideon, and you're going to lead us to victory. Tell me what happens, won't you?"

"Of course," Gideon said. "I have to think—I'm not sure—"

"I understand," said Joash. He slapped his son's back and left him alone to think and prepare.

Gideon paced. What should he ask? What was reasonable? What would be definite—something so simple he could not mistake the answer? Something fitting?

He opened his mouth, and words to God poured out: "If you will save Israel by my hand as you have promised—look, I will place a wool fleece on the threshing floor. If there is dew only on the fleece and all the ground is dry, then I will know that you will save Israel by my hand, as you have said."

Gideon had raised his hands while speaking, and now he dropped them, not sure whether to feel hopeful or frightened or foolish or something else entirely. But what was said was said, so when evening came, he picked out a fine coat recently sheared from one of his sheep. He checked the fleece over, to make sure it had no imperfections, and then brought it to the threshing floor.

Tuesday morning, Gideon awoke early. The memory of the fleece struck his brain like lightning, and he was up and running before he was properly awake.

Gideon arrived at the threshing floor in no time. He juddered to a halt at its edge. Was the fleece still here? Yes— right there. This was it.

Gideon stepped forward. The floor was dry, and his sandaled feet kicked up dust as he walked. He knelt beside the fleece and touched it. It squelched with water.

Gideon hesitated, and then stood and fetched a large bowl. He set the bowl on the floor and picked up the fleece, which was thick and heavy with water. He squeezed the fleece over the bowl. Enough water poured out to fill the bowl until it slopped over.

When he'd wrung out every drop, Gideon sat back on his heels, letting the damp fleece fall on his lap. The LORD had provided a miracle.

Or has He? whispered a voice in the back of his mind, one that sounded a lot like Judah's. *Wool always holds water better than dirt. What if the dew simply sank in already? What if you're only seeing what you want to see, regardless of reality?*

"All right," Gideon said to himself. "I'll ask for one more sign—that's reasonable, isn't it? I have to make absolutely sure."

To God, he said, "Do not be angry with me. Let me make just one more request. Allow me one more test with the fleece, but this time make the fleece dry and let the ground be covered with dew."

Tuesday morning flew by, swiftly followed by the afternoon. As more and more Israelites arrived, Gideon kept busy by organizing them into groups by tribe and clan, under clan leaders known to them. He assigned others to make sure the men had food, weapons, tents, and other supplies. He didn't know what God's battle plan was, but whatever it was, he intended to be ready.

That night, Gideon could hardly sleep. He set the second fleece out before going to bed, and spent several hours counting sheep in his head. But at last, he fell into a light drowse and then a deeper sleep, and he did not wake until the next morning.

When he did wake, Gideon again bolted upright and ran for the threshing floor. This time, when his foot hit the threshing floor, it sank into dark, sticky mud and left footprints behind. He squelched over the mud, the hair on the back of his neck prickling, and bent to touch the fleece.

It was bone dry.

CHAPTER TWELVE

Phantoms in the Dark

The children's bellies ached with hunger and their throats screamed for water. They sucked their own saliva, but they could not quench their terrible thirst.

They'd been holed up in the Stronghold since Sunday afternoon—two full days. Last night, Benjamin had again snuck out to see if there was any way to escape, only to find there were more Midianites around than ever. He had nearly gotten caught stealing a half-empty flask of sour wine that burned in their throats and made them lightheaded.

"We should have tried to get past that patrol, trap or no trap," he told the others in a gloomy rasp. "It was our one chance."

Samuel shrank under these words, as if trying to shove himself into the walls of the stronghold. He'd taken to fingering the Egyptian knife he'd found and thinking up desperate, heroic, terrifying plans he was sure wouldn't work. He wasn't a warrior. He couldn't imagine killing one full-grown man, let alone dozens and dozens.

Would being caught by the Midianites be a worse death than thirst? He wished he knew. But either way, he wasn't ready to die yet.

Leah could see how depressed the boys were getting. As

the eldest, she felt it was her responsibility to come up with a plan, but what could one girl do against this enemy?

Nothing. She could only be brave for the boys' sake and hope something would happen.

Then something did happen. Up until then, the Midianites had been wandering all over the valley, making scattered camps, more and more of their allies streaming in and making it more and more impossible to escape. Then, late Tuesday afternoon, the sounds outside the Stronghold changed. The children heard shouted orders and a great deal of clattering and shuffling around, not to mention grumbling:

"I can't believe we have to fight alongside the Amalekites. What was King Zalmunna thinking?"

"Don't let anyone hear you say that. You know what the Wolf does to dissenters."

"I'm not a dissenter! Don't you tell anyone that! I'm surprised—that's all. I have the highest respect for King Zalmunna. A man has a right to be surprised."

"Yeah, yeah. You going to do your share of the pickup?"

"Picking up is for servants. These hands are made for killing Hebrews."

"You've got that right. It's past time we spilled the blood of those pesky shepherds."

The children had no choice but to listen to this unpleasant talk, but soon it turned to something much more hopeful for them:

"What's the name of the place we're going? Mobek?"

"What do you care about Hebrew names?"

"Stuff it up your nose. Just tell me what the stupid hill's called."

"Stuff it up your own nose."

"Peace, you two. I don't want to listen to your bickering. And it's Moreh, for your information."

"Moreh!" the children mouthed to one another in pleased realization. Moreh was a hill in the valley north of them. Several miles north, in fact. If the whole army really was going there, the children would be free to leave any time they wanted.

It had been awful, waiting without hope of escape; but in some ways, it was even more awful after they had hope. They listened harder than ever, waiting for the noise to decrease, to demonstrate there were fewer Midianites around.

At first, they couldn't hear any difference, any evidence that the Midianites were actually leaving to go north. But after a couple of hours, the sounds grew less: the footsteps disappeared into the distance, and the rattling of metal faded entirely. The moon had gone down and all was dark and silent under the glistening stars.

"It must be safe by now," Benjamin whispered.

"Let me go first, to check," Leah whispered back. She felt slightly ashamed of letting Benjamin head out first last time, so she dove for the crawlspace without waiting for a response.

Outside, a fresh breeze refreshed Leah. It felt so *good* to be out of that ruin! She stretched, cautiously looking around.

A shuffling behind her made her spin, but it was only Benjamin crawling out after her.

"I told you to wait!" she hissed.

He shrugged and put a finger to his lips, which made her scowl. Her scowl deepened when she saw Samuel following Benjamin out. Why didn't boys ever do what they were told?

It was too dark for Samuel to see her scowl properly, but he felt it. He ducked his head in response, but he didn't apologize. He wanted to be out of there as badly as the other two. And it was safe now, right? He crept after his friends, around one wall and then another, keeping low in the ruins.

"Over here," growled a Midianite voice.

The children shrank against the wall, horrified. Samuel made to scramble back into the Stronghold, but Leah held him firmly, afraid of any noise.

"You're sure the others have all joined the camp?"

"Sure I'm sure. Idiots. Hurry up. I want some good loot before we leave there. There must be something in these ruins."

Leah shoved her knuckles between her teeth and held her breath. She could see the glow of their lanterns as the men neared. They were trapped.

Samuel felt strange and wobbly. He instinctively clutched his golden knife again. He'd have to be very fast if he was going to use it. Should he give it to Benjamin? He licked his lips.

As he neared complete panic, another idea came to him—an idea, and a memory. Those two Midianites who'd camped by them the first night, the ones who had heard their voices—they had thought they were ghosts.

Those Midianites had been superstitious. Might these two be, also?

"After this, we should move on to that town west of here," said one of the Midianites.

"Fine by me—but let's finish searching these ruins first. They just *look* like a place Hebrews might hide treasure."

"Assuming it hasn't already been found."

The enemy was nearly here. This was Samuel's only chance. He licked his lips again, then pursed them and made the most ghostly sound he knew: a singing whistle. His voice vmmmed low while the whistle blew high, like the sound of wind through a canyon.

Leah tried to hit him to make him stop, but he moved out of reach, creeping through the ruins.

"What's that?" asked one of the Midianites suspiciously. "What's that noise?"

"It's only the wind. Shut up and keep looking."

"Nyusah, nyusah, nyusah," Samuel whisper-sang nonsensically, and then let out a high, unearthly screech.

Benjamin caught on to what he was doing and crept in the opposite direction, snickering audibly, his laugh growing louder and wilder.

"That's not the wind," said the Midianite, drawing his sword with a *shick* of metal on metal.

Samuel's voice cut off in surprise, but Leah motioned him vigorously to keep going. She'd realized what the boys were doing; and if they stopped, the game was up.

Pitching her voice high, she sang breathily. "Come-come-come-come to me." Benjamin laughed crazily and Samuel whistled.

One Midianite said uncertainly to the other, "Gobel said this ruin was haunted. You don't think—"

"I never listen to Gobel."

"Come to me, come to me," Leah sang, and then her mad laughter joined in Benjamin's, piercing two octaves higher.

The Midianites had had enough. Cursing vile filth, they turned on their heels and bolted.

Leah stopped laughing and looked to Benjamin and Samuel. That had actually worked! She could almost start laughing again—only in relief!

A slow clap interrupted her triumph.

"Well done," said a stranger with hard eyes and a drawn sword. "Very clever. But it won't be enough to save you."

CHAPTER THIRTEEN

Too Many Soldiers

"The LORD said to Gideon, 'You have too many
men.'" (Judges 7:2)

By Wednesday evening, every fighter from Asher, Zebulun,
and Naphtali had arrived. That was the good news. The bad
news came when the scouts reported that the Midianites were
almost ready to move. Gideon couldn't wait any longer; it
would be disastrous if the Israelites were caught unprepared.

Gideon had never much minded speaking in front of a
group of people, but this time his stomach jiggled with nerv-
ousness. He wasn't speaking only to his fellow Abiezrites,
people who had known him all his life. The heads of three
other tribes and numerous clans were gathered on a hillside
above him as he stood on the speaking stone. These great
men were looking to *him* for guidance!

No, he told himself. *It's not about me. They are looking
to the* LORD *for guidance.*

First his father would greet the men. "Tell them of God's
promise," he urged Joash. "Tell them of the miracle of the
two fleeces."

"I already have," Joash said confidently. "By now, everyone's heard the story—from the grim-faced veterans to the most trembling newcomer. They are waiting for you, my son. They are ready. Trust in the LORD."

Gideon looked over the heads of the leaders to the crowd of troops. Tens of thousands of them, some proud and tall, some laughing nervously. He felt a rush of pride and gratitude that these people, these strangers, would come to his people's aid. That they would trust him to lead them.

It was time. Gideon motioned for silence. "Three hundred years ago, Moses led our people out of Egypt without ever raising a sword—because he had the LORD on his side. Forty-seven years ago, Judge Deborah and Commander Barak faced odds worse than the ones we go against now—but they trusted the LORD and so they triumphed.

"Now, we face a new challenge. Our enemy has a hundred thirty thousand men to our thirty-two thousand. Our enemies have camels, and we are on foot. Difficult odds. Might be impossible odds, if numbers were all that mattered.

"But we have the LORD on our side, and His help is worth more than every man and camel in the land. Not through our own power, but through the power of the LORD, we will be victorious.

"We will win, just as Moses and Joshua and Deborah won! The LORD will wipe out our enemies. They will never destroy our crops again. We will no longer have to hide like voles in the field." Gideon punched the air with his next three words: "Strength! Faith! Victory!"

"Victory!" cried Joash, pumping his fist. Several others followed Joash's lead, but not all of them. Gideon had done his best, and the belief of many was great—but looking them over, Gideon realized that his earlier pride was misplaced. Many still doubted, including more than half the leaders. They would follow him because they were desperate—not because the LORD had promised to deliver them.

This was a sobering thought, one Gideon couldn't simply shrug off. He could only hope the mood would improve by the time they had to fight.

And that God would reveal His battle plan soon....

Clouds hung heavy, damp, and chilly. Only at the horizon did a golden glow mix with the morning mist, adding warmth to an otherwise colorless morning.

Flowering grass, soaked with dew, slapped Gideon's thighs and tickled his hands as he arrived at his new camp, above the base of Mount Gilboa. From this angle, the enemy army, some four miles north, near the hill of Moreh, was hidden from view by gray distance and sprouting trees.

Gideon didn't need to see those soldiers again. The sight of them, from the top of Mount Gilboa, was fixed in his memory: a horde of Midianites, like a swarm of flies, blackened the valley. His scouts who had managed to get close enough had reported in detail about the men's heavy armor, their personal strength, their camels, their unmatchable weapons...

Gideon wondered once more as he walked, *What is God's plan?*

He glanced over his shoulder. Following him down the mountain came his army. They looked pretty impressive from this angle, he had to admit, despite their hodge-podge accoutrements. If he didn't peer too closely, he couldn't see their fear, their uncertainty, their inexperience.

Gideon beckoned for them to join him. He had stopped most of the way down the mountain, near where a large, shallow cave gaped blackly on the sunlit hillside. Inside the cave, the spring of Harod gushed pure, cold water. Outside the cave, the water flowed gently into a flat meadow and then streamed down the slope as the Harod River.

Armies had camped here before, and caravans commonly stopped beside Harod's clear water. In this hot, dry land, water could be more precious than gold.

Gideon smiled, the smell of the water bringing nostalgic memories to mind. When he'd been a boy, he and his friends had often come here on hot summer days and splashed around for hours.

Of course, that had been in a time of peace, before the Midianites had come....

Gideon stood at the edge of the cave, hands on hips, and watched his army arrive: thirty-two thousand men. *We aren't such a small force,* he told himself, *and we know the land.*

We can do this.

Joash wasn't with him at the moment, so Gideon had to imagine what his father would say. Maybe, "They clearly respect you as a leader, my son." Gideon's chest swelled with pride.

That was right; they trusted him. Of course they did. He was their Judge. He, of everyone, had been called to save them. He was Jerub-Baal, and he would lead them to victory. And then?

Then, they'll make me their king. I'll be far greater than even my father. They'll sing songs about me and tell their grandchildren about my miraculous victory.

It was a glorious thought, and Gideon basked in it. He turned from his army and looked north. The morning was clearing, and he could again see the Midianite army, below them and a couple of miles off. Sure, the Midianites were alarming, but the Midianites didn't have Gideon. He would bring his people to victory.

"You have too many men."

Gideon started at the voice—a voice out of heaven. The LORD was speaking to him!

God went on, "I cannot deliver Midian into their hands, or Israel would boast against me, 'My own strength has saved me.' Now announce to the army, 'Anyone who trembles with fear may turn back and leave Mount Gilead.'"

Gideon immediately felt ashamed of himself. This was what came from thinking boastful thoughts! He'd better wipe them from his mind and just humbly obey God.

But... send away part of his army? Who even knew how many men would leave!

God knew, of course. God knew exactly what He was doing. His use of Gilboa's ancient name, Gilead, reminded Gideon of Scripture. In Deuteronomy, just before a battle, God had instructed army officers to say, "Is any man afraid or fainthearted? Let him go home so that his brothers will not become disheartened too."

Gideon hated to send away any of his forces, when they were already so outnumbered. But then, he thought, *Surely most of them will stay with me. I'm the Judge. The LORD has chosen me to bring us to victory. He called me a mighty warrior! Maybe this is only to prove that no one will leave.*

This thought pleased Gideon, and it was with a light heart that he called together the clan leaders and told them magnanimously, "The LORD has spoken to me. He has said that any man who trembles can leave. Tell your men! We don't need anyone who is afraid of the coming battle."

The clan leaders looked at him incredulously, but Gideon was the head of their army. Maybe he had a plan. So they shrugged to themselves and went to obey.

Curious to see what would happen, Gideon secretly followed one of the clan captains from the tribe of Zebulun.

"Stop a minute, fellows," the captain said. "Judge Gideon's made an announcement: anyone who doesn't want to fight can go home. You won't be punished as deserters, but you're out of the action."

"Truly?" asked one man, a muscled and middle-aged fellow whom Gideon thought would be a great asset to the coming conflict. "We can just leave?"

"You can just leave."

The man jumped to his feet with a laugh. "Best news I've ever heard! This fight looks worse by the minute. You coming?" He looked to his friend.

"You bet I'm coming. They outnumber us four to one! I'd like to be breathing tomorrow, thank you very much."

"What's wrong with you?" a third soldier asked them, a lean eighteen-year-old herdsman. "You cowards, or something?"

"More like we're no longer reckless youths," said the first man. "Listen, Jared, you can stay if you like. But if Gideon doesn't need me, I'm going back to my family. Why shouldn't I?"

Jared's face darkened in anger. "Because we came all this way to drive these nomads out! Let's do it and get it over with. Who knows when we'll have another chance?"

Another man spoke up. "If you want to fight, good for you. But as for me, I'm going back home to finish harvesting before the Midianites attack us there."

Jared folded his arms. "Well, I'm not afraid of Midianites or anyone else, and I'm staying. You can go huddle at home like rabbits if you want." He raised his sword in a salute to the clan captain. "I'll see you at the spring!"

He strode down the hill, angry and proud. The men he left behind were embarrassed, but that didn't stop them from returning uphill to safety—and then packing up their belongings to hike back home.

Gideon retreated from his listening point, abashed. How many times would he have to learn the same lesson? "Forgive me for my pride, O God," he said. "I will rely on You. I will not again forget who the real leader of this army is! Please, do not send away any more."

But that wasn't the end of it. The news of his announcement spread like wildfire, and by afternoon, 22,000 Israelites had packed up and left. Instead of 32,000 men against 130,000, Gideon was left with only 10,000.

It's what I deserve for being so proud, he told himself. *God is testing my faith—and the faith of my people. I must be strong. If he can deliver us with 32,000, surely he can deliver us with 10,000. That's still a lot of men.*

Come to think of it, defeating the Midianites with so few men would just make him look the more impressive!

Hardly had that thought occurred to Gideon, than God spoke again: "There are still too many men. Take them down to the water, and I will thin them out for you there. If I say, 'This one shall go with you,' he shall go; but if I say, 'This one shall not go with you,' he shall not go."

God wanted to send away *more* men? Gideon was stunned. But he had promised himself that he would have faith and rely on the LORD and not his own pride. So instead of questioning God, he hurried to obey.

When Gideon again called the clan leaders together, he could see their sideways glances at him, like they were afraid of what crazy thing he might order next.

Well, let them think what they liked. He wasn't going to let feeling embarrassed stop him from obeying the LORD.

"Bring your men to the water," he said, "and the LORD will choose from among them."

This was exactly the sort of thing that the leaders feared, but they'd come this far. Even more, they were brave and loyal men, and like Gideon, they had made a choice to trust God. They were not going to change their minds now. Most of them immediately turned to obey. Most of them…but not all.

One of the generals from Asher argued angrily, "There's nothing wrong with any of my soldiers. They're as brave and strong as any in Israel. You'll be sorry if you try to fight without them."

"This isn't about me," Gideon said truthfully. "I may be Judge, but the true general of this army is God—and the general is the one who chooses whom to send into battle. Have faith."

"We will," said a Naphtali general. "We trust you, Jerub-Baal—and we trust in the LORD. Come on; let's do what he says."

Gideon watched the clan leaders go off and talk to their men. He wondered how God would choose only certain soldiers without making one man resent another, or one clan angry at another. He'd seen petty resentments build into lifetime hatreds.

As Gideon waited for instructions, his soldiers arrived at the bank of the river. It was a hot day, and most of the men immediately got down on their knees or bellies and began drinking.

Again, the LORD spoke to Gideon: "Separate those who lap the water with their tongues as a dog laps from those who kneel down to drink."

Gideon blinked and looked over the men. Of course, men who knew one another stayed together. The tribes formed groups along the stream, and in each group, men of the same clan bunched together. Most of the men got down on their knees to drink, but a few here and there lay on their stomachs. They filled their cupped hands with water and drank it, just like dogs when lapping water. Gideon chose one of the prone men and tapped him on the shoulder.

"Go and pick out all the men who lap the water up, like you do," he said, "and pull them aside."

The man was puzzled, but he did as he was told.

There seemed to be no pattern to how the men drank: sometimes, two or three together stood and lapped water from cupped hands. Other times, Gideon's assistant had to walk a long way to pick them out. The men he selected came from every tribe.

All told, only three hundred men lapped up their water like dogs. The man Gideon had sent gathered them off by the side to await orders. They didn't look like anything special, to Gideon. What was he supposed to do with them?

Then the LORD spoke to him again: "With the three hundred men that lapped I will save you and give the Midianites into your hands. Let all the others go home."

Really? Gideon thought. He shook his head—not in negation, but in amazement.

If God delivered them from 130,000 enemy soldiers with only these 300, no one could doubt the Israelites had won by God's power.

Even the Amorites would see the LORD is the true God, Gideon thought. *There will be no real Baal worship after this!*

Gideon took a deep breath, and drew the attention of the nearly 10,000 men who'd knelt at the river to drink.

"All of you in this area are to return to your tents and wait there for more orders," he announced. "We may have another battle coming, one over in Gilead, so be ready. Leave trumpets and supplies here for these 300 men."

The 10,000 men looked at one another, confused. Many of them had seen how Gideon chose his men, but they couldn't fathom how Gideon could use these 300 soldiers.

Scouts? Archers? It didn't make sense, but most of them shrugged to themselves. They didn't mind resting a little longer.

While they were leaving, Joash joined his youngest son. "I'm proud of you," he said. "I wish I had been as faithful to the Lord as you are now. I wish I had never built that altar to Baal, never let your brothers worship at it. I can't change that, but I'm glad you're doing the right thing."

With those words, Joash embraced his son, turned, and began the long trek back up Mount Gilboa.

CHAPTER FOURTEEN

Into the Fire

The stranger advanced, his sword swishing back and forth with every step. The children lurched back, looking around wildly for a way to escape. But the stranger had chosen his angle well: they were trapped against a corner, with no way to go but up.

With his usual agility, Benjamin was atop the crumbling wall in a flash. He offered his hand to Leah, and she scrambled up next to him.

Samuel wasn't so lucky. He was the farthest from the wall, and terror made him clumsy. While he was still grasping for handholds, the stranger swept forward like a dark shadow, sword flashing.

"Don't kill me!" Samuel squeaked, shrinking down into the corner of wall and ground.

The stranger arced his blade down, until the edge rested a scant inch from the boy's throat. "You're Hebrews," he said.

Samuel gulped. The man reeked of camel and old sweat. He didn't look like the typical Midianite, because he wasn't: this man was an Amalekite—a member of a tribe even the Midianites despised.

"We're not going to tell you anything!" Leah squeaked from atop the wall. "Not even if you kill us!"

Easy for you to say, Samuel thought. *It's not you he's about to kill!*

The Amalekite grinned at them, showing a pair of golden teeth. "We'll see about that," he said, grabbing Samuel by the hair.

"Run!" Samuel squeaked to the others. It was probably the bravest thing he'd ever said, but it didn't do him any good: when Leah and Benjamin jumped down the opposite side of the wall, they found another Amalekite waiting for them.

This Amalekite was even bigger than the other one, and he hadn't bothered to draw his sword. He simply grabbed each child with one hand and tucked them under his arms, carrying them like bags of flour.

Benjamin and Leah kicked and struggled and shrieked. They totally forgot about staying silent so they wouldn't attract more enemies. But no matter how they writhed and scratched, the big Amalekite didn't let them go. In fact, he hardly seemed to notice their struggles.

The first Amalekite, who seemed to be the leader, jerked his head at the second and dragged Samuel by the hair north across the grass... toward the Midianite camp. "No!" Samuel cried. "Please no!"

The Amalekites threw the children atop their camels, holding on with iron grips.

It was two miles to the southern end of the camp. Leah felt sick, slung across a camel like this. And Benjamin was slung half on top of her, which making the ride even worse.

What were the Amalekites going to do to them? She wished she'd never left the hiding place.

Benjamin was much subdued. This wasn't what adventures should be like. Not bumping along on a camel. Not scary. He might die.

The forty minutes it took the camels to cross the distance from the ruins to the Midianite camp seemed to take forever.

At the Amalekites' command, the camels knelt near a campfire. The men pulled the children off roughly and threw them down near the fire.

Benjamin crawled slowly to his feet and looked around. Twenty enemy eyes looked coldly back at him, and ten swords reflected firelight. He looked behind him and saw the two Amalekites who'd captured them.

"What are you going to do to us?" Leah asked. Benjamin thought she was trying to sound brave, but her voice quavered and squeaked. Samuel, at her feet, only sat and cried, tears and snot streaming down his face.

"Hebrew children," announced the first Amalekite—the leader.

"What did you bring *them* for?" asked another man. "Hebrews are for killing, not capturing. Look at them— useless!"

"You're an idiot, Ali," said another man. "What their parents won't tell us, the children will! What do you think about that, children? Tell us what you know and die quickly or live as slaves. Don't tell us… " He grinned, licked his lips, and fondled a small knife. "And we have fun."

Samuel gasped for breath. Leah covered her mouth with her hands, her eyes round as coins.

Benjamin, by contrast, was having a sort of epiphany. Brand new ideas were racing, exhilarated, through his brain. He had a hard time not grinning when he said, "You want to know about us? About our soldiers and things?"

"Don't you dare tell them!" Leah cried. "Don't you *dare*, Benjamin!"

"If I don't, they'll kill us," Benjamin replied. He knew objectively that he was terrified, but tingling energy was running up and down his arms. He felt he could sprint a mile and not get tired. "It doesn't matter what they do to us—Gideon will destroy them."

"Gideon," an Amalekite muttered. "I know that name."

"Of course you do," Benjamin said brightly. "He's the mighty warrior who captured your two spies."

"Benjamin!" Leah hissed. "Shut up!"

"If the girl interrupts again," said the Amalekite leader, "kill her. Now, boy, tell us all about this Gideon fellow. What has he done before? What are his feats? What battles has he won?"

"Oh, lots," Benjamin said airily. "Every battle he's ever fought. He's a brilliant strategist, of course. Let's see. There was that time, last spring, when about twenty bandits tried to waylay him on the road. He was all alone except for one servant who was crippled and could barely see. Gideon wasn't even armed at the time. In fact, he had nothing to fight with except an ancient threshing fork..."

Benjamin stopped and coughed. "Ugh, it's hard to tell stories with all this smoke around, when I already have a sore throat. If only I had some water!"

"Oh, give him some," growled one soldier. "Get on with it, boy."

Benjamin sipped the water demurely and then passed the flask to Samuel, who guzzled.

"Yes, a threshing fork," Benjamin continued. "He'd already been threshing for hours, so you'd think he'd be tired, but Gideon's not made of any ordinary flesh and blood. You see, he has the Israelite God on his side...."

In the hot, smoky little camp, surrounded by filthy, heavily armed men, Benjamin launched into his fantasy. The more he said, the more Benjamin got into it. Some of his story, he made up on the spot, but as for most of it—well, he'd spent years dreaming *he* was a mighty hero. He accidentally said "I" instead of "Gideon," several times, but his audience didn't seem to notice. The Amalekites sat agog, listening to his tales of Gideon. They seemed to forget that he was their prisoner as the night wore away.

When morning came, they stopped him to confer among themselves. Benjamin hardly had to hint at it before they provided all three children with breakfast.

Leah had spent most of the night watching Benjamin with a combination of fascination and exasperation. What was her brother doing? Didn't he know this was serious?

Yes, and he's saved our lives by telling these stories, but this won't last forever.

Shame crept up on her. She was the eldest! She was the one who was supposed to save them!

You still have to. Benjamin is buying you time, but sooner or later, the Amalekites will get tired of his stories, and where will you be then?

It was a sobering thought, and Leah had plenty more time to think it, because when daylight came, the Amalekites began taking the children around to the other camps, to share Benjamin's stories. Leah and Samuel were sometimes called upon to confirm them, which they did almost mutely.

By afternoon, it seemed like half the camp had heard Benjamin's stories, which were growing wilder and bolder with the hour. Some soldiers—not just Amalekites anymore, but other tribes too—started asking Benjamin about stories he hadn't made up, but Benjamin elaborated them anyway, turning rumor into fantasy and back into rumor.

Oh, Benjamin, she thought. *Don't run out of stories, not yet. And don't get caught lying, or they really will kill us!*

CHAPTER FIFTEEN

Dreams and Portents

"During that night the Lord said to Gideon, 'Get up, go down against the camp.'" (Judges 7:9)

The rest of Thursday passed in a blur. All but Gideon's chosen three hundred men retreated up the mountain to safety, to wait for a battle.

Gideon paced, waiting for God to tell him what to do next.

As night fell, the Midianite camp, instead of disappearing into gloom, transformed into a galaxy of campfires bright and vast as a city.

Gideon's camp, by contrast, was invisibly black. "No fires tonight," he had ordered. "Let them see only darkness all around them. Let them wonder why we don't have fires and where in the darkness we lurk. I want them nervous."

Also, then they can't see how few of us there are.

Maybe the Midianites would still think he had thirty-two thousand men. Maybe they'd assume even more had arrived. It might give his men an advantage.

Gideon briefly considered having each of his three hundred men light a fire—light ten fires, spread out—to make it look like they had so many more than they did. But if that was going to be his tactic, he should have done it back when he had enough men to create something impressive. Thirty-two thousand men each lighting ten fires—now that would scare the invaders!

The LORD will tell me his plan, Gideon reminded himself. *I just have to wait and trust.*

But it was hard to trust when he looked at his people's odds and was afraid. He scolded himself, but still he felt like he had a belly full of snakes.

Shaking his head, he forced himself to stop pacing and go lie down on his mat and try to sleep.

Midnight came, and Gideon had just drifted off when the LORD's voice woke him: "Get up, go down against the camp, because I am going to give it into your hands. If you are afraid to attack, go down to the camp with your servant Purah and listen to what they are saying. Afterward, you will be encouraged to attack the camp."

Gideon didn't think he'd ever get used to having God speak to him. Who could? The LORD knew his thoughts and heart better than he did, even without Gideon saying a word. Not only that, but the LORD accepted Gideon's weakness and encouraged him.

"I am afraid to attack with so few troops," Gideon answered. "I trust you, LORD, and even though I'm afraid, and I don't see how this can work, I will go."

He got off the ground, excitement wiping away fatigue, and went to shake Purah awake. He put one hand over his servant's mouth, so Purah wouldn't make any noise, but he needn't have worried. Purah had stayed close by just to be ready to help his master, and he knew how to stay silent.

Purah opened his eyes and looked up at Gideon. Though the night was dark, he recognized his master by the feel of his hand and the smell of his breath. When Gideon beckoned him to follow, he did not hesitate or complain.

Under the sparkling starts, Gideon led Purah across the dark meadow, stepping carefully to avoid the sleeping shapes on the ground. *What an odd army this is,* he thought. Usually, the Israelites fought alongside fellows they'd grown up with, staying in their clans or villages and following a trusted local leader. But Gideon's men had been chosen by how they sipped water, not what town they came from. Most of them didn't know one another, and many had never heard of Gideon before he'd summoned them to fight. What they all had in common was that they were Israelites, descendants of Abraham, Isaac, and Jacob; followers of the one true God; and defenders against the Midianites.

During the previous day, Gideon had gone to much effort to learn as many names as he could, and now that effort paid off: he remembered that the two men on watch were called Jared and Reuben.

They're not much older than my son Jether, he thought, with a tinge of sadness. Jared was watching east of here, but Reuben wasn't far off. Best let him know what was going on.

Reuben turned as he heard their footsteps. Gideon couldn't see his expression, only the brightness of his eyes. "Who comes?" he called in a breathy whisper.

"Gideon and Purah." Gideon stepped close enough to see the shadows of Reuben's face and kept his voice low. "Report."

"No action, sir," Reuben announced. "No sight or sound of Midianites anywhere near our camp." Unable to resist, he added, "I hope we're going to attack soon, sir. From here, the enemy will head right up to the Plains of Esdraelon, into Zebulun. My tribe. Last year, they ruined our whole wheat crop and killed most of the livestock. We survived the winter on barley."

Gideon thought about his own farm. Barley was the first grain to ripen and was harvested at Passover. But barley was mostly used as animal food; only the poorest people ate it.

He was glad he'd gotten most of his wheat crop in. No doubt, anything he'd left behind had already been stolen or destroyed.

Reuben went on, brimming with excitement. "Look at all those campfires down there! The Midianites are all bunched together in one place, ready for us to smash them in one blow. When do we do it?"

Purah stepped forward to interrupt. "I doubt our three hundred swords will be the solution; God will provide a miracle—like he did for Moses, Joshua, and Deborah. Maybe a flash flood—or an earthquake—or a plague."

Reuben grinned. "A plague of venomous snakes, I hope. Or maybe crocodiles, to eat them up."

Gideon listened with interest. He wasn't about to tell them that he had no idea what the LORD planned. He said vaguely, "You'll be amazed what God can do with only three hundred men."

"I already know what he can do," Reuben said. "Remember when Abraham rescued Lot from four kings and their combined armies? Abraham only had 318 soldiers. He divided them into three companies and attacked at night. The enemy soldiers were caught off guard, and they panicked and ran away!"

"I'd forgotten about that," Purah mused. "Only problem is, how can we fight with swords and spears in the dark? We couldn't tell friend from foe. We'd be as likely to kill our fellow soldiers as the enemy! No, what we need is a miracle."

"Or Abraham," said Reuben to himself. Then he caught

Gideon's eye and hurried to correct himself: "But we have our own Judge! Those Midianites are going to regret ever coming here!"

A rustling in the bushes fifty feet away stopped their conversation. Something was moving around out there in the darkness. Gideon strained to make out a shape in the dim starlight. He heard soft steps. Whatever or whoever was out there would have heard their voices and would know exactly where they were. If he only had a bow and arrow...

"Follow me," Gideon whispered. He didn't dare split up his little group—as Purah had pointed out, they might accidentally attack one another in the dark. Instead, he moved soundlessly to a new location twenty feet from the first one. Then he waited and watched.

The bushes rustled again. What was out there? Midianites, preparing to attack? A prowling lion?

A shape moved against the starlit sky. A deer! Then another. A little herd of four deer, their necks high, stepped daintily from the bushes to the stream.

The three men laughed, but Gideon secretly felt foolish. Here he was, a leader, supposed to be brave—and he was afraid of a few deer!

"A reminder," he told Reuben. "Purah and I are going. I grew up around here, and I know every foot of the land. After I return, you'll get your wish: we'll attack."

"Sir!" Reuben exclaimed. "You can't go—you might be caught and killed—and we can't afford to lose you. Not just before the battle!"

"You don't understand," Gideon said. "This isn't a whim: the LORD is sending me. I'm meant to hear something there. I came to you, not to ask you to take my place, but to make sure you don't hurl your spear at me when I return."

Horrified at the idea, Reuben quickly said, "I'll be careful, sir!"

Gideon nodded to him. Reuben stiffened into military alertness, then nodded back, honored.

There was one advantage to paring down his troops to three hundred, Gideon reflected: they all trusted him utterly.

No. They all trusted *God* utterly. Which was far more important.

This thought echoing through his mind, Gideon crept stealthily down the slope to the valley, Purah right beside him. Careful and alert, they avoided dangerous or rocky spots where they might slip, making a noise. Both knew their mission wasn't dangerous. On a dark night like this, the only way they'd find a Midianite spy was by tripping over him. Only Gideon's faith, courage, and bull-headed determination kept him going forward, straining eyes and ears for danger.

The closer they drew to the Midianite camp, the more Gideon wondered why they hadn't spotted more patrols. He'd only seen a few men walking back and forth, and those stopped to lazily chat. Definitely not what he'd expected in an army.

"Where do you think the guards are?" Purah breathed in his ear.

Gideon shook his head in the darkness. Then he understood. "We keep forgetting," he murmured back. "This isn't a real army—it's just a bunch of barbarians. They must not be organized at all."

Encouraged, they snuck in closer, Gideon leading and Purah following several paces behind. Gideon had no idea where he was going, but he trusted God to lead him.

They stayed in the trees as much as possible, stepping quietly. Then, at last, the trees cleared in such a way that they could see the camp spread out before them.

It was much worse than Gideon had imagined. Tents

filled the northern valley as thickly as locusts on wheat fields. Gideon could no more count their camels than he could count grains of sand on a beach. There was no trace of the farm that had stood here for decades.

"Is *this* supposed to make us feel better?" Purah whispered miserably.

"The LORD said to listen to what they say. Come on—and hush!"

They snuck up close to a tent and crouched in its shadow. Voices were speaking inside, one upset and one nervous. "I don't want to go back to sleep! I don't like this!"

"None of us like it," snarled the anxious voice from inside the tent. "Close your eyes and start snoring; it'll be over soon enough."

"You don't understand," the first man insisted. "I'm not being unreasonable. I had a dream. A round loaf of barley bread came tumbling into the Midianite camp. It struck the tent with such force that the tent overturned and collapsed."

There was a moment of tense silence. When the second man responded, he sounded as nervous and unhappy as the first. He said, "This can be nothing other than the sword of Gideon son of Joash, the Israelite. God has given the Midianites and the whole camp into his hands."

Gideon half fell over from shock. He withdrew just into the shadow of the trees and then bowed down in worship. Joy, hope, and courage coursed through his limbs as he silently cried out, "Oh, great God, thank you! We are in your hands! Instruct me, and I will do whatever is your will!"

No verbal response came to him this time, but understanding covering him like a cloak.

He knew exactly what he had to do.

Gideon signaled to Purah, and they ran back to the camp, heedless of enemy eyes. No one could spot them when God was on their side.

Purah was laughing by the time they arrived back. "A prophetic dream sent to a Midianite!"

Gideon grinned. "Barley bread for Israel and tents for the desert peoples!"

"And the sword of Gideon—don't forget that."

"A sign if ever there was one. I wonder how they learned my name."

"Probably those spies we set free. Who else?"

"And to make themselves look good, they called me a mighty warrior," Gideon said, shaking with amusement. "I guess they'd be ashamed to say an ordinary farmer captured them."

They were almost back now, and Gideon called ahead of him, "Reuben! Reuben, wake everyone and bring them to listen. We attack tonight!"

"Ahead of you, sir," Reuben called back. "Behold your army!"

Gideon crested the last hump before the spring of Harod, and the dark hillside resolved itself into three hundred figures, sitting and waiting for him.

He laughed again, so elated he couldn't wait for introductory talk. "Praise the LORD!" he cried, in a voice all could hear. "Get up! The LORD has delivered the Midianite camp into your hands!"

He motioned his soldiers upright. "We have been to the Midianite camp. They have seen our thirty thousand men coming down the mountain and going back up again, as if changing shifts to drink at the river. They have heard my name, and they have heard the name of the LORD.

"In battle, in the dark of night, what matters is not what's true, but what the enemy believes. The LORD will destroy them through their own fears! How magnificent is the wisdom and the power of the LORD! Praise be to God!"

"Praise be to God!" his army shouted back in one rush of exhilaration. "Praise be to God!"

CHAPTER SIXTEEN

Piles of Gold and Jewels

Nightfall returned, and the children were still alive. They had been fed again, and Benjamin lolled like a king on the cushions the Amalekites had provided. He was excessively pleased with himself, although his voice was hoarse and his throat sore from so many hours of storytelling.

Leah gripped her hands together until the knuckles went yellow. While Benjamin had been enjoying the attention, she had come up with a story of her own. Now, she was only waiting to tell it.

One by one, the Amalekites lay down to sleep. They didn't leave anyone on watch; they simply tied up the children so they couldn't escape.

That suited Leah perfectly. She waited until the Amalekites' breathing evened out and then called the name of the one she'd chosen: "Timek. Timek, wake up."

Timek's eyes opened. He was one of the older Amalekites. His camel was hung with gold baubles, and gold replaced most of his teeth. Despite his already being wealthy, Leah had noticed the way his eyes followed the others' possessions, and how he, more often than any of the rest, had asked Benjamin about Israelite treasure.

Each time he'd asked, Benjamin had snorted and said, "What treasure? You people have been raiding us for the past seven years; we have nothing left. Of course, Gideon is going to change all that...."

But Leah had seen Timek hadn't been satisfied with this answer.

"Timek," she called again, "I want to make a deal with you."

The Amalekite bared his golden teeth at her. "You think I care where your mommy and daddy are holed up like shivering voles? I don't. They can stay there until they rot. There's nothing you can offer me."

"I can offer you treasure, Timek. Piles of gold—ancient gold from distant lands. Gold no one else knows about."

Timek snorted, but his eyes gleamed bright with greed, and he got up to come close. His breath stank of old meat, and dirt engrained his pitted face. "There is no gold left, girly. Your boyfriend made that clear."

"My brother," Leah said primly, "was telling the truth—as far as he knew it. There is no Israelite gold left. But there is Egyptian gold. I found it. And I'm willing to lead you to it."

Timek's eyes narrowed. "You lie."

"I can prove it. Samuel"—she didn't have to prod the boy; he was awake and staring. He hadn't said a word since their capture—"give him the gold knife."

Timek's eyes sharpened on the word "gold," but he remained cautions. "Don't you go pulling out a knife," he warned Samuel. "You tell me where it is, and I'll get it."

Resentful, but too afraid to argue, Samuel pointed to his pouch. The Amalekite grabbed it with one hand and slashed off the straps with a twitch of his sword. Not taking his eyes off the children, he dumped the pouch over the ground.

Samuel's treasures scattered: colorful stones, dried flowers (now crushed), an interesting twig… and, glorious in the middle, the elegant shape of an ancient blade.

Timek sucked his breath between his teeth in a greedy whistle. He sheathed his sword and plucked up the knife, turning it over and over in his grubby hands.

Samuel tried to shrink back further, but the Amalekite shot him a look, and he froze.

"Now, now, now," Timek said slowly, "this *is* interesting. You say there are more of these?"

Samuel opened his mouth to say "no," but Leah beat him to the punch: "There sure are, sir. I found them when I was exploring the caves. I gave one to Samuel as a present, but he doesn't know where it came from. Only I know."

Benjamin tried to elbow her to warn her not to give away the secret of the caves, but Leah dodged him. It was her turn to save them.

"We were telling the truth about all the Hebrew treasure being gone, but there are piles and piles of this stuff. If we show you," she added cannily, "you'll let us go—right?"

"Oh, sure," said the Amalekite. "I'll let you go."

"Of course," said Leah thoughtfully, "we'll have to go secretly. The cave is on Mount Gilboa, you see. If anyone sees us sneaking there, they'll get a share of your treasure. I have a deal with you, but I don't have a deal with them."

"And when you get there, you think you can run off while I'm not looking," said Timek. "Think that if you like, but you'll find I'm not that stupid." He tied the knife sheath onto his belt. Then grasping the knife with one hand, he grabbed Samuel by the hair with the other, hauling the boy upright and pulling him close. Samuel cried out in pain, tears coming to his eyes, and then tensed as the edge of the golden blade flashed close to his face and stopped near his throat..

Timek grinned. "Go on," he told Leah. "Lead the way. Just remember that if any of you try to escape or warn anyone, your friend's blood will be on your hands."

"We won't try to escape, sir," Leah said humbly as Timek cut her bonds. She rubbed her wrists and climbed slowly to her feet. She swayed slightly as the circulation returned, but she didn't have the luxury of time. Any of the Amalekites, snoring around the fire, might wake up at any time. And what would happen if they spotted the children leaving? Everything would be ruined. "It's this way."

For the most part, the Amalekite was content to let Leah lead. She walked quickly but carefully, checking behind her shoulder every few seconds to make sure the others were staying close, and beckoning when they strayed too far.

Had the children known anything about armies, they would have found something strange here. For though there were tens of thousands of soldiers not far to the north, there were almost no patrols. Many of the campfires had left no one to keep watch, and not a single sentry stopped and questioned their small group. True, the Amalekite camp was on the edge of the main horde, but all the more reason to be careful.

Of course, there was a good reason for this: the Midianite army wasn't a proper army at all, only a horde of desert warriors who spent most of the year fighting each other. They only banded together when they attacked the Israelites.

Timek wasn't any more eager than the children to be seen by other Midianites, lest he have to share his treasure. So, like them, he was careful, and he only relaxed when they left the camp and headed toward Mount Gilboa.

Benjamin, by contrast, became jittery. He had no idea what was going on, and he didn't like it. Unlike Samuel, he didn't have a knife to his throat, and Leah could guess he might try jumping the Amalekite to save Samuel.

"Don't do anything stupid," she warned him in an undertone, catching him by the arm. "You must trust me."

He looked at her with wide, wild eyes.

"Hey, now," Timek said roughly, "don't go whispering ahead of me like that. You stay quiet, or you talk loud enough for me to hear—got it?"

Samuel squeaked as the knife drew a line of blood from his throat.

"Got it!" Leah said quickly, and glared at Benjamin until he grudgingly said the same.

That ought to keep Benjamin in line for a little while. They still had more than a mile to go.

Leah kept walking, west and north—too far north to lead them anywhere near the hiding Israelites. She'd thought briefly, desperately, about leading this man into the village and hoping her people could overwhelm him, but she didn't see any way to manage that without Samuel being killed. No, she'd stick to her original plan.

"This way," she whispered, leading the Amalekite up the foot of the mountain. It was hard to find her path with only the dim glow of starlight, and several times she missed a step and jolted her thigh or scraped her hand on a rock.

The Amalekite had to sheathe the knife and use his free hand to help him climb, but he didn't let go of Samuel for a moment. "Is it much farther?" he growled.

"Oh, no," Leah said. "Not much farther. Just ahead."

"Then stop for a moment," Timek said. "There's a good tree here. Take this rope and tie up the boys—and do a proper job of it. If we don't come back to untie them, they can starve... or wait until the army gets here." He grinned at her and licked his gold teeth. "Personally, I'd prefer starvation."

Leah shuddered but obeyed. Under Timek's watchful gaze and ready knife, she took the rope and tied Samuel and Benjamin to a tree. She didn't know any trick knots, and she wouldn't have dared try them if she did. Benjamin glared at her and Samuel stared in shocked incomprehension, but she couldn't spare any comforting words. She could only hope that her memory from a year ago was perfectly accurate.

It should be. She had once boasted that she knew the cave system better than anyone else.

It was time to put her nightmares to good use.

"Lead on," Timek said when she was done. He motioned with his sword. "Show me the treasure."

"Leah—" Benjamin said urgently, trying to communicate with her—but what, she did not know.

"Be quiet," Timek snapped. "Show me the treasure, girl."

Heart thumping wildly, Leah bowed her head. "Yes, sir," she said humbly. She could see Benjamin still trying to communicate with her, but she knew what she was doing. She crawled over the rocky ground. Where was the entrance? Not there, not there—ah!

It looked smaller than she remembered, darker.

Timek grunted, seeing he was going to have to crawl.

"May I have the lantern?" Leah asked humbly. "Then you wouldn't have to try to hold sword and lantern."

Timek laughed. "Nice try, girl. You aren't going to lose me in the dark. Get on with it."

"Yes, sir," Leah said. Secretly, she sighed with relief. She hadn't wanted the lantern, but it would have seemed strange not to ask. So she ducked her head and crawled into the narrow lip of the cave.

It had been a long time since she had done this sort of thing regularly, but she hadn't forgotten. Now, if only everything were like she remembered...

Leah kept going, hyper-conscious of the man behind her, but concentrating on something else. As the cool cave-smell enveloped her, she pricked her ears, listening for the subtle, nearly silent sound of slithering, the movement of a nest. Last time, it had been right through—there.

She licked her lips. She was sweating heavily.

She slowed her movements, made them subtle and gliding and as quiet as she could. The Amalekite behind her grunted with effort as he crawled along on his forearms, swearing to himself. He was having trouble with the smallness of the cave, she realized. Maybe she could lead him to a spot too narrow for him to get through and escape that way...assuming he didn't chop her feet off as she went.

No. This was best. She turned into the side passage and sped up, careful to keep her movements smooth and silent.

Timek sped up too, swearing and grunting more than ever, the hilt of his sword clanking against rock, the lantern swinging.

Leah got into the more open space before him and immediately rolled off to the side, to a dark corner where he couldn't see her.

Timek pulled himself out after her. It was high enough in here for him to stand if he bent over. He shone the lantern around stomped deep into the space, far past where she huddled near the entrance. "Where are you, you stupid—agh!"

Leah covered her mouth to stifle her cry. The memory of Bithiah flooded back to her, of dragging the snake-bitten girl out of the cave, of being unable to save her.

The Amalekite was yelling, and his yelling attracted yet more mole vipers.

Leah stayed motionless in the corner, suppressing her trembling and silent sobs. She waited long enough to be sure, and then forced her seized-up muscles to move, to take her back through the tunnel and toward freedom.

The Amalekite's screams chased her out.

CHAPTER SEVENTEEN

Torches and Trumpets

"The Lord has given the Midianite camp into your hands." (Judges 7:15)

Gideon rushed back and forth, sizzling with energy. He grabbed armfuls of trumpets and shoved them at his men, all the while crying, "Jars! I need empty jars!"

Purah raced after him, trying to tell him where the jars were, but Gideon couldn't stop long enough to listen. "Get him jars!" Purah yelled at a handful of men.

Bemused, the men jogged off to obey.

"No, no!" Gideon cried. "A torch for every man; a jar for every man. Torch in your left hand; jar in your right. Use your jar to cover your torches—good. Everyone have torch and jar?"

Everyone had one. Gideon ran up and down the line, double checking until he was satisfied. Then he planted himself. He had broken his men up into three groups of a hundred men each—as Abraham had done: one he would lead, and one under each of two other commanders. Aside from torch and jar, each man was fully armed and armored, with a trumpet strapped to his side. The light of excitement shone in every eye, and not a few men grinned at one another, wondering what Gideon had up his sleeve.

"Watch me," he told them. "Follow my lead. When I get to the edge of the camp, do exactly as I do. When I and all who are with me blow our trumpets, then from all around the camp blow yours and shout, 'For the LORD and for Gideon!'"

Gideon lit his torch, then shared the fire with Purah, who shared it with the men next to him. Each man hurriedly hid his lit torch under his jar. If any distant Midianites had been watching, it would have looked like a few fireflies flicking into existence... and then vanishing again, like figments of the imagination.

Gideon crept down the mountain as swiftly as he could move without tripping. His hundred men stayed close to him, and the other two groups fanned out—one to the left and one to the right. They quickly made it down to the base of the mountain, where smooth grass silenced their footsteps. An alert patrol might have spotted them... the Midianites had no patrols, only a few sleepy guards near the tents.

Gideon and his hundred soldiers reached the edge of the camp at the beginning of the middle watch, just after the Midianites had changed the guard. The previous watchmen had tumbled tiredly into their tents, and the newly awakened ones were groggy and grumpy. Many of the rest of the Midianites had drunk heavily the night before and were now deeply asleep. No one expected an attack.

Gideon smashed his jar against a rock, revealing the torch, lifted his trumpet, and blew. His hundred men were barely a second behind him. A cacophony of terrifying noise swept over the Midianite camp—pottery smashing and trumpets blowing. Then the trumpets fell silent for a moment, and three hundred voices shouted, "A sword for the LORD and for Gideon!"

In the Midianite camp, Commander Zeeb was sleeping peacefully. He dreamed he was a real wolf and the Israelites were sheep. In his dream, he led a pack of slavering wolves up a mountain, each one set on tearing apart Israelite children.

As his wolf form ran up the mountain, a great noise surrounded him and terrible lights. They were everywhere, surrounding him. The sheep had transformed into men with grim faces and sharp swords, descending on him from every direction.

Commander Zeeb liked to think of himself as fearless, but he jolted awake in sudden terror. Thick smoke filled his tent, and from outside came the clang and shouting of battle. The Israelites were attacking! Zeeb grabbed his great sword and rushed out in his night clothes. Burning torches in the night blinded him, and he bared his teeth and snarled.

A blurry, dark figure spotted him and raised its sword. Zeeb ran at the man, swinging his own sword, and killed him. "Die, Israelite!" he yelled, and plunged ahead into the fray, slaughtering everyone who came toward him.

In another part of the camp, Commander Oreb crouched, his raven hair in disarray, his gold earrings and pendants missing. The whole world seemed to have gone mad. Everywhere he looked, he saw fallen Midianites. The Israelites must be everywhere, to have killed so many of his men. There must be tens of thousands—hundreds of thousands of attackers!

He gritted his teeth. One man ran at him, screaming. Oreb lunged out of his refuge and hurled his spear. When the man was dead, he grabbed the spear and retreated back to his hiding place. He'd loot the body later. Right now, he had to concentrate on not letting anyone get too close.

Panic reigned in the Amalekite quarter. "It's Gideon! It's Gideon!" one man cried. "We're being attacked! We're all going to die!" He spun around as a dark shape ran at him, sword waving. Without a moment's hesitation, he lunged forward with his own sword, skewering his attacker. "The mighty warrior has come to kill us all!"

"He said 'Gideon'!" shouted another man, his face lost in the screaming, stabbing, slashing darkness. "He's an enemy! Kill him!"

"They're everywhere!"

"We're going to die!"

"Run!"

On the outskirts of the camp, yelling and blowing their trumpets, the Israelites watched in fascination as the Midianites killed one another while being convinced they were killing Israelites.

"The LORD has brought madness to our enemies!" Gideon cried. "Even as they terrorized us, so they are killing one another in their terror!"

Not a single one of the Israelites had been killed; not one had even breached the outer ring of the camp. They stayed at the edges and stomped pottery and blew trumpets and shouted as their enemies destroyed themselves.

Up on Mount Gilboa, the ten thousand men Gideon had sent back watched in confusion. The whole Midianite camp seemed to be in uproar, although it was impossible to see what was going on from this distance. Had Gideon been captured? Killed? The men burned to go down and help, but obeyed their orders.

"Even if it's not time for us to fight yet," they said to one another, "we'd better get ready. Look, there they go!"

The Midianite camp was breaking south, fleeing.

"Could Gideon have done this with only three hundred men?" one Israelite said wonderingly.

"No," said another, "but the LORD could. Have you seen where I put my spear? Thank you."

Waiting was hard, but they didn't have to wait much longer: a messenger came running up the mountain.

"The Midianites are retreating!" he panted. "Judge Gideon summons you to help him chase them out! We're winning!"

The ten thousand roared with delight and flooded down the mountain like a tidal wave.

Hardly any of them noticed, as they passed, three exhausted children climbing back up to their homes, to be hugged and scolded and hugged again by their mothers.

Another messenger rode at top speed to the hill country of Ephraim, calling to anyone who would listen, "Come down against the Midianites and seize the waters of the Jordan ahead of them as far as Beth Barah."

The people of Ephraim had been tormented by the Midianites for as long as the other tribes had. Within an hour, every man who could fight had grabbed his weapons and run to cut off the enemy. They blocked the Midianites' path to the south and killed any who tried to get past—including Commanders Zeeb and Oreb.

Zeeb, who had taken such pleasure in hunting down and killing Israelites, was killed at a winepress. This winepress was afterwards called the Winepress of Zeeb. Oreb, who killed to get treasure, died near at a large rock, which afterwards became known as the Rock of Oreb.

And onward, the Israelites chased the Midianites.

CHAPTER EIGHTEEN

Finish It

"Gideon and his three hundred men, exhausted
yet keeping up the pursuit, came to the Jordan
and crossed it." (Judges 8:4)

At first, Jether was happy and flattered to be included in the
ten thousand men helping Gideon chase the Midianites. He
felt ashamed of himself for freezing during the ambush of the
two spies, and wanted another chance to be a hero.

When the messenger had come up Mount Gilboa and
shouted that the Midianites were fleeing, Jether had grabbed
up a sword, face flushed with excitement. He had run in the
midst of the men all the way down to the valley. Most of the
Midianites were already far ahead of them, and Jether hardly
saw an enemy, let alone had to fight one.

I'll get my chance, he told himself. *I'll avenge my brother and everyone else those monsters have murdered!*

Before long, the ten thousand caught up with Gideon and
his three hundred. Not a one of the three hundred had been
killed.

"Father!" Jether cried, seeing Gideon's tall, princely form.
"I've come to fight alongside you!"

141

Gideon caught his voice and grinned over at him. "I'm proud of you, son," he said.

Jether flushed with pleasure and fingered the hilt of his sword. He trotted over to his father and walked at his side. Together, they strode at the front of the Israelite army.

As his initial excitement wore off, Jether discovered that chasing Midianites was tiring. Never once did they stop—it was always on, on, hurry, hurry, and no one seemed to have brought any food.

Finally, Gideon called his army to stop at a town to ask for help. At this town, Succoth, Gideon demanded, "Give my troops some bread; they are worn out, and I am still pursuing Zebah and Zalmunna, the kings of Midian."

The officials of Succoth smirked at him. They had heard all that had happened, including that Oreb and Zeeb had been killed. Sarcastically, they said, "Do you already have the hands of Zebah and Zalmunna in your possession? Why should we give bread to your troops?"

Gideon flared with terrifying fury. Jether cowered back from him, astonished to find his father so frightening. But Gideon didn't care. His men were hungry, and it was his duty to look after them. He snarled at the town elders, "Just for that, when the LORD has given Zebah and Zalmunna into my hand, I will tear your flesh with desert thorns and briers."

Jether looked at his father in alarm, but Gideon only stormed on, his army behind him, to a second town, Peniel. When the elders of this town also refused to help, Gideon told them, "When I return in triumph, I will tear down this tower." Then he stormed on, after the Midianites.

Jether trotted alongside his father, wondering if Gideon actually meant to carry out his threats. By this time, the boy was so exhausted that he wished he had stayed at home.

"Can't we go back now?" he asked Purah. "The Midianites are running away—we've won."

The servant smiled gently at him and shook his head. "We haven't won," he said, "not as long as the Midianite kings are still alive. Don't you see? If we let Zebah and Zalmunna escape, they'll come back next year with another army—and you can bet they won't fall for the same trick twice."

"Oh," Jether said quietly. "But what if we can't catch them?"

"The LORD will help us," Purah said, and left it at that.

In fact, it wasn't that many hours later that a messenger came riding up to Gideon. Jether was too far away to hear what the messenger said, but he saw a look of delight spread over his father's face. A few minutes later, Gideon gathered his generals and made an announcement.

"We've cornered them!" he shouted, his voice hoarse with fatigue but his eyes bright. "They're in Karkor—and there are only fifteen thousand of them left. A hundred and twenty thousand have fallen!"

A moment of stunned disbelief followed this announcement, and then a cheer started up. The weary Israelites became reinvigorated. They shouted and stomped their feet so excitedly that it took Gideon five minutes before he could calm them down enough to speak again.

"We'll take the route of the nomads east of Nobah and Jogbehah!" Gideon told them. "They won't be watching that way—they'll never see us coming."

Here it is, Jether thought, adrenaline coursing through him, wiping away his exhaustion. *This is my big moment.*

"Stick with me, kid," Purah told him. "I'll look after you."

Jether nodded. "I'm ready," he said.

What happened next, Jether would never forget—but it

was never quite clear either. He remembered clearly how the Israelite army snuck up the nomads' route, following Gideon's commands, and then suddenly broke upon the Midianites. But after that followed an hour of confusion and violence. Some of it was vividly clear in Jether's memory: flashes of color, especially the red of blood. Other parts blurred into a smear of terror and confusion.

True to his promise, Purah stayed beside the boy, protecting him. Together, they fought. Fortunately, Jether didn't freeze up this time. He didn't have time to think at all; he was too busy staying alive.

And then, abruptly, it was over. The Midianite kings broke and ran, and what was left of their army ran after them.

"Don't let them get away!" Gideon yelled. He could have saved his breath: two dozen Israelites immediately surrounded the kings.

Zebah and Zalmunna looked at each other and immediately dropped their swords and raised their hands. They knew when they were captured.

The battle was over.

When the rest of the Midianites had died or fled or thrown down their swords and surrendered, Gideon came over to the kings. But he didn't speak to them, not yet. He hadn't made up his mind what to do with them. He simply looked at them and then left again, to speak to his army.

"Here, we rest," Gideon announced. "In the morning, we move again."

Another ragged cheer went up. Flushed with success, the Israelites set patrols to protect themselves and then lay down to sleep on the ground.

"Well done, lad," Purah told Jether. "We've won."

Jether smiled tightly at the servant and put his head down. But he didn't sleep. His hands were shaking. He felt like he had been hurt inside, like his mind had been cut up by the swords that had never touched his body. He felt sick and more frightened than ever.

I hate war, he thought. *I hate it; I hate it. I just want it to end.*

Around him, he could hear the slow breathing of soldiers settling into sleep. He tried to close his own eyes, but the darkness frightened him more than anything.

It's like having a nightmare while you're still awake.

Morning came none too soon for Jether. Finally, they could go home! He wanted to see his mother again and his sisters. He wanted to rest, safe, in the comfort of his own home.

But though Jether had forgotten about his father's threats, Gideon had not. As the Israelites marched back north, they stopped at the two towns that had refused to help them. At Succoth, Gideon had the captured Midianite kings pulled forward.

He proclaimed: "Here are Zebah and Zalmunna, about whom you taunted me by saying, 'Do you already have the hands of Zebah and Zalmunna in your possession? Why should we give bread to your exhausted men?'"

Gideon turned to his men. "Drag out the elders of the town, and we will punish them with desert thorns and briers."

Jether covered his eyes and tried not to watch.

Next, Gideon dragged his army over to the town of Peniel. "Tear down the tower," he ordered his men, "and kill everyone inside."

This started Jether shaking again, and he had to fight not to cry.

Purah patted his shoulder. "You're being very brave," he said encouragingly. "Your father will deal with the kings next, and then we'll go home."

Jether nodded, sniffing, and straightened his back.

Hardly had he recovered himself than he saw Gideon coming toward him, smiling a feral smile his son had never seen before. "Come with me, Jether," he said. "Let's go talk to some kings." He slung his arm over Jether's shoulder, and they walked together to where the prisoners were kept. There, Gideon let go of his son and had Kings Zebah and Zalmunna brought forward.

Interested, Jether forgot his fear long enough to look them over. Both had somewhere found actual armor, as if they hadn't been woken in the middle of the night. The fatter one wore bracelets of gold, but the taller was more sparsely dressed.

Really, Jether thought, *they just look like people. Have they been the ones causing so much trouble? I wish they hadn't.*

"Zebah and Zalmunna," Gideon said thoughtfully. He too was looking at them with interest, but his eyes were hard. "Tell me, what kind of men did you kill at Tabor?"

The two kings glanced at each other. The taller one was defiant, proud. The short, fat one had an eager smile on his face, ready to please. "Men like you," Zalmunna said briefly, scornfully.

"Each one with the bearing of a prince," Zebah said in his most flattering voice.

It was the wrong thing to say. Gideon's face, already cloudy, darkened into a storm. "Those," he said, each word crisp and angry, "were my brothers, the sons of my own mother. As surely as the LORD lives, if you had spared their lives, I would not kill you." He turned in one sharp, angry movement to Jether. "Kill them!"

Jether started. His eyes flickered between Gideon and the

kings. "Wha—what?" he asked, taken aback.

"Kill them!" his father ordered again. "For many years, you have begged for a chance to revenge yourself upon the Midianites. Now is your chance: here are the kings. Here are the men who have made us suffer for seven years. And I give them into your hands. Kill them!"

Jether looked again between his father and the kings. He obediently put his palm on the hilt of his sheathed sword, but he didn't draw it. His whole arm felt weak and his knees quaked. *Kill them*, he told himself. *Draw your sword and kill them.*

He felt like he was going to start crying again. He didn't want to kill them or anyone. He was so frightened. He just wanted this to end.

"Pathetic," said the shorter king to his friend.

Zalmunna snorted. "Come, do it yourself," he told Gideon scornfully. "'As is the man, so is his strength.'"

Gideon looked again to Jether, but he could see the boy was in no state to help. So he drew his own sword.

The kings saw the intention in his eyes, and both drew themselves up, ready. A second later, Gideon lunged forward, killing first tall Zalmunna and second stout Zebah. The kings fell to the ground, dead.

As his army watched, Gideon then went to the kings' camels, which had been captured alongside them. Dangling on the camels' necks was gold—gold stolen in years past from Israelites. Gideon unlooped chains of gold from the camels' necks and held them high.

"The looters have been looted!" he cried.

"Hurrah!" the soldiers cried. "All hail Judge Gideon!" they cried. "Jerub-Baal! Victory!"

Gideon grinned around at them and bowed, but they weren't done. He didn't see who started it, but soon, the Israelites were shouting, "Rule over us—you, your son, and your grandson—because you have saved us out of the hand of Midian!"

When Gideon heard this, his smile vanished. Their words exactly echoed his own fantasies several days before.

He wasn't about to fall into the trap of pride again; he'd learned his lesson. "I will not rule over you," he said, "nor will my son rule over you. The LORD will rule over you."

> "Thus Midian was subdued before the Israelites and did not raise its head again. During Gideon's lifetime, the land enjoyed peace forty years." (Judges 8:28)

No One's Perfect

Grandmother Leah breaks off, looking into the distance as she remembers these times long past.

"Thank you for the story," you tell her. "By the way, I think you were very brave, luring Timek into the cave like that."

Her eyes brighten, and she laughs. "The funny thing is," she says, "I haven't been afraid of a cave since!"

"Or a snake?"

"Well," she admits, "maybe I'm a little afraid of snakes."

You smile at one another, but there's something else niggling at you. After Gideon, there was peace. Forty years of it! There isn't peace anymore. Musing about this, you say sadly, "If only our Judges were like Gideon! They seem so weak in comparison."

Grandmother Leah starts to agree and then stops. "No one is perfect, dear," she says gently. "Not even Gideon."

"I guess he was a little mean to Jether," you admit.

Grandmother Leah is shaking her head. "Maybe, but that's not what I meant. You see, I didn't exactly tell you the whole story, because the rest of the story makes me so sad. The truth is that after Gideon defeated the Midianites, he used some of the gold he plundered to make an ephod—that's a special sort of priestly breastplate—which he placed in Ophrah—in this very town." She sighs, as if it hurts her to say the next part. "And they started worshiping it. Even Gideon, who knew better, started worshiping the gold ephod as an idol."

You can hardly believe your ears. "But that's silly!" you say. "He knew better! The LORD spoke to him in person!"

"I know," Grandmother Leah says, "and I'm glad you recognize it." She pats you on the shoulder. "Let that be a lesson to you, young one. No one is perfect—except the LORD."

You straighten your back, your eyes bright and your voice sure. "I," you say firmly, "will never worship an idol. I will always follow the LORD—no matter what."

And you do.

Made in the USA
Middletown, DE
02 January 2024